PATHS
OF FAITH

Edited by
Elizabeth J. Harris

Christians Aware

Our Thanks

–   to the London Central Mosque for permission to use the photograph on page 57;

–   to the Bahá'ís of the UK for the photographs on pages 7 and 12;

–   to the Jain community in Leicester for the photograph on page 35.

Contents

Preface

Christians Aware is delighted to publish 'Paths of Faith' in partnership with the Committee for Inter Faith Relations of the Methodist Church. We offer the book as a resource for Christians who wish to learn about other faiths and to meet their people.

Each chapter of the book is written by a different person. The chapters on the Bahá'ís and on the Zoroastrians are written by members of those faiths. The other chapters are written by Christians who have specialist knowledge and experience of the faiths and of their people. All the writers offer their work as bridges towards understanding, trust, friendship and working together between people of faith in Britain today.

We have published this book in the spirit of ' Faith Awareness,' the inter faith programme of Christians Aware. In our programme we offer opportunities for encounter between members of all faiths in the hope that participants will seek to develop mutual understanding, not hiding differences and recognising the uniqueness and special contribution of each faith to its people and to the world. We trust that this book will be a contribution towards the development of the understanding and friendship we hope for and work for. We may all be enriched by learning about the faiths of our neighbours and in working with them in the community.

In learning about other faiths and in meeting the people we may be helped by the words of Max Warren:

'Our first task in approaching another people, another culture, another religion, is to take off our shoes, for the place we are approaching is holy. Else we may find ourselves treading on another's dream. More serious still, we may forget that God was there before our arrival.'

Barbara Butler
Christians Aware

Introduction

These articles began their life as a series in *The Methodist Recorder* at the end of 1998. For nine weeks, they took up the centre spread. Not all readers liked it. Some could not understand why a Christian newspaper should present other faiths in a sympathetic way. To them, the presence of the articles in such a prominent position spoke of compromise, threat, even syncretism. But the positive responses outweighed the negative. The *Recorder* was praised for being brave, innovative and helpful. After all, the Methodist Conference of 1994 had adopted eight principles on dialogue and evangelism, the third of which said, 'Opportunity must be given to Methodists to learn about the beliefs and practices of people of other faiths.' What could be more obvious than that the Methodist newspaper should help in this task of educating!

Now, the hope of the contributors is that their words will have a wider audience, among Christians and beyond. Yet, it must be remembered that the original target audience was Christian. The authors were chosen with this in mind. For, they were not only asked to convey information about the faith concerned but also to raise issues relevant for Christians and to challenge the negative stereotypes that, in some Christian writings, have born false witness to the richness of the world's spiritual heritage. And since the idea for such a series arose within the Methodist Committee for Inter-Faith Relations, several of the writers were consultants within that Committee.

To communicate, accurately, the heart of a religion in less than three thousand words is an almost impossible task. No religion is a monolithic entity. Every faith has changed and adapted throughout history, some more than others. As a result, most faiths hold diversity within themselves - diversity in practice and ritual, institutional structure and, in some cases, doctrine. Dialogue on issues of orthodoxy and orthopraxis, doctrine and action, happens within faiths as well as between them. Yet, in spite of diversity, in each faith, there is an underlying unity, an underlying spirit and character which motivates and inspires. It is this that the authors have tried to capture. Much is left out. Generalizations have had to be made.

Each author has approached the task in his or her own way. Absolute uniformity of structure was not insisted on. The only guidelines that were given were that the following should be included: information about the beliefs and practices of the religion; data about its presence in Britain; relevant hints for Christians when approaching the faith; and useful addresses and books. Using this, the authors have stamped the articles with their own personalities and experience. So Nick Sissons has chosen to concentrate on Jews in Britain whilst Eric Lott, when dealing with Hindus, has focussed on what is encountered in India. Some authors have placed their major emphasis on doctrine, whilst others have taken a more sociological approach.

The book can be used in a number of ways. For some individual inquirers it may serve as a leaping off point for further travel and exploration, either in meeting people from the faiths concerned or in picking up further reading material from the suggestions given at the end. For others, it may simply open a window to the fact that Britain is a multi-religious country and that there is much that is good and worthy of respect within the faiths of others.

The book also lends itself to group use. Some of the authors have appended questions that a group might like to tackle. Where there are no questions, the following may help get groups started:

Were you surprised by anything you have learnt and, if so, why?

In what you have learnt about the faith concerned, is there anything that resonates with your own religious beliefs or experience? If so, what?

Is there anything that jars with your own faith or that causes you difficulties? If so, what?

Has the faith challenged you in any way? If so, how?

What extra information would you like?

Have you met a person from the faith you have been studying? If so, has the chapter helped?

Discussing a chapter using these questions could be a good preparation for inviting a member of the faith concerned to your group or for visiting a local place of worship.

We hope that this book will help Christians and others discover the holy, the wholesome and the inspirational outside their own faith. We hope it will go some way to demonstrating that inter-faith understanding is no longer an optional extra. It is a necessity. The religions of the world are not the same. They speak of different goals. They look to different teachers and different texts. A word used in one tradition may have a different meaning when used in another. Encountering such difference can be disturbing but it can also be enriching and challenging if we use it to look anew at our own faith. Woven into the difference are also numerous touching points. Faiths touch in the longing in each for goodness, wholesomeness, righteousness or obedience, and for that which transcends materialism, consumerism and selfishness. Faiths touch in their concern for a peaceful society where all have enough to flourish, to grow and to explore. It is to exploration that this book invites you.

Elizabeth Harris
Secretary for Inter-Faith Relations
The Methodist Church

Chapter One

The Bahá'ís: turning to the transcendent God

John Barnabas Leith

The Beginnings of the Faith

Mid-nineteenth century Persia was not a good place for spiritual and religious renewal. This poor and backward-looking society, largely dominated by a powerful class of Islamic clergy, did not welcome new ideas and religious innovation was often violently suppressed. Yet it was in this milieu that the Bahá'í Faith had its beginnings.

In the 1840s and 1850s, a prophetic movement, growing from the teachings of the Báb (the Gate), swept Persia with the idea that a new dispensation, a new era in human existence, had arrived and the way was being prepared for 'Him Whom God shall make manifest'. One of those who became a leading member of the new movement was Mirza Husayn-Ali, known to the world as Bahá'u'lláh (the Glory of God). In the summer of 1852, during a period of persecution of the Báb's followers, he was arrested and cast into a notorious dungeon, known as the Síyáh-Chál or Black Pit, deep beneath one of the city squares of Tehran. Bahá'u'lláh was incarcerated for four months in this terrible place, formerly the sump of a public bath. He later described it as 'a place foul beyond comparison' and says, 'God alone knoweth what befell Us in that most foul-smelling and gloomy place!'[1]

What befell Bahá'u'lláh in that place was an experience of revelation that taught him that he was indeed the one foretold by the Báb, 'He Whom God shall make manifest'.

Bahá'u'lláh and his family were expelled from their native land in January 1853, never to return. Forty years of imprisonment and exile took him to Baghdad, Constantinople, Adrianople (present-day Edirne in Turkey), and finally to Acre, the ancient crusader city in the Holy Land. It was in April 1863, at the end of his stay in Baghdad, that he first announced his mission to a few of his chosen followers. While in Adrianople he began to compose an extraordinary series of epistles to the kings and rulers of his time, commanding them to work for peace and care for the poor. Bahá'u'lláh's eventful earthly life drew to its close in a house just outside Acre in 1892.

Teachings from God

So, what made Bahá'u'lláh so dangerous that he was forced to spend most of his life in exile? Well, firstly he claimed that what he said was of God, and he challenged his hearers to accept the sacrifice that he had made for the peoples of the world:

> The Ancient Beauty hath consented to be bound with chains that mankind may be released from its bondage... He hath drained to its dregs the cup of sorrow, that all the peoples of the earth may attain unto abiding joy, and be filled with gladness.[2]

Secondly, he called humankind to turn to God, to live a life of true piety and service, to acquire the virtues that we need in both this life and the next. Each of us, says Bahá'u'lláh, has twin duties: to recognize God's messenger for the day in which we live and to 'observe every ordinance of Him Who is the Desire of the world'. 'These twin duties are inseparable. Neither is acceptable without the other.'[3] God calls us and we respond with our recognition, our love, our wholehearted obedience to God's law, and our devoted service to God through our service to our fellow humans. Thus we receive the gift of salvation.

Bahá'u'lláh asserted that God has spoken to humankind periodically throughout history. A series of Manifestations of God – the founders of the great faith traditions – had revealed God in their lives, their words, their very beings, and had renewed what Bahá'u'lláh called 'the changeless Faith of God, eternal in the past, eternal in the future'.[4] Each Manifestation had two 'stations' or aspects: the 'station of distinction' in which each had a distinct individuality and mission; and the 'station of essential unity', in which all their utterances 'are in reality but the expressions of one Truth'.[5] Through these Manifestations, God has progressively educated his children until we now stand on the threshold of that great and irreversible transformation to our collective adulthood. It is to this transformation and the subsequent development of a planet-wide civilization – based on the clear and deeply held understanding that 'The earth is but one country, and mankind its citizens'[6]– that Bahá'u'lláh addressed much of what he said.

God's infinite essence is beyond our knowing and yet Bahá'u'lláh bade us know the unknowable. However, Bahá'u'lláh, in his mercy and loving kindness, taught that the Manifestation of God is like an absolutely clear mirror in which we may see reflected what we can know of God, His qualities and attributes. Thus we learn to encompass a paradox: that God, who is utterly transcendent is 'closer to me than my life-vein'.[7]

Everything Bahá'u'lláh taught was infused with his abiding sense of the transcendent oneness of God, of the essential oneness of the human race, and of the oneness that underlies all religion. 'So powerful is the light of unity,' says Bahá'u'lláh, 'that it can illuminate the whole earth.'[8] All the messengers of God come from the same source; they 'have been sent down, and their Books were revealed, for the purpose of promoting the knowledge of God, and of furthering unity and fellowship amongst men.'[9]

The Religion Spreads

From its beginnings as a seemingly insignificant offshoot of Shi'a Islam, the Bahá'í community began to spread in the East and, towards the end of the nineteenth century, in the West, firstly in the United States. From America the Bahá'í teachings spread to Britain and Europe. In 1911 and again in 1912–13 Abdu'l-Bahá, Bahá'u'lláh's eldest son and the Head of the Bahá'í community, made two epic journeys to the West. He travelled North America from coast to coast, lecturing and teaching. In Britain he visited London, where he gave his first public address in the West, Bristol, Oxford, Liverpool, Edinburgh and Woking. His presence deepened the Bahá'ís' understanding of Bahá'u'lláh's teachings and stimulated them to new levels of activity.

Bahá'ís in Britain

The British Bahá'í community took many years to grow to its present size, but the British Bahá'ís were actively engaged in the work of their new faith from the early days, and the National Spiritual Assembly, the national governing council of the community, was first elected in 1923. It was one of the first National Assemblies to be established in the world.

Things have moved on a long way since then. Local Bahá'í communities are active all over the UK (and, indeed, all over the world). Each community with nine or more adult members elects a Local Spiritual Assembly every year to administer its affairs. There are now more than 180 Assemblies throughout the UK as well as a number of smaller communities. Groups of communities form units each year to elect delegates to the National Convention, where the National Spiritual Assembly is elected. Every five years, the members of National Assemblies from all over the world converge on Haifa in Israel, site of the Bahá'í World Centre, to take part in the International Convention and elect the Universal House of Justice, the Bahá'í world governing council.

The Bahá'í Life of Faith

As a religion without clergy, the Bahá'í faith depends on the active involvement of its members in all aspects of the community. The heart of the faith is the individual's relationship with God, nurtured by prayer, meditation and an annual fast. Bahá'u'lláh's writings include many prayers and meditations for personal use, prayers that express our longing for and devotion to God and testify to our relationship with our Creator. Every Bahá'í who has reached the age of spiritual maturity, fifteen years, should recite one of three "obligatory" prayers each day. This is the shortest of the three:

> I bear witness, O my God, that Thou hast created me to know Thee and to worship Thee. I testify at this moment to my powerlessness and to Thy might, to my poverty and to Thy wealth. There is none other God but Thee, the Help in Peril, the Self-Subsisting.

Bahá'ís must also feed their souls by reading from Bahá'u'lláh's writings each morning and evening. It can be a few words or many; it doesn't matter so long as the beauty and meaning of the words sink deep into hearts and souls. Bahá'u'lláh teaches that the meanings of the Word of God are endless. Heart and mind are God-given instruments to fathom the deeps of the ocean of God's Word. 'Ponder in thine heart,' says Bahá'u'lláh as the prologue to many of his utterances. He also says that an hour's meditation is preferable to seventy years of 'pious worship'.

The Bahá'í Faith is not a sacramental religion nor does it have liturgy in the way that exists in some Christian churches. Bahá'í collective worship, whether in community or family or other gathering, is essentially very simple; it revolves around reading from the prayers and writings of the Báb, Bahá'u'lláh and 'Abdu'l-Bahá. These readings may be elaborated with music and other art forms, but no particular form should ever be allowed to become a required ritual. Bahá'ís sit down together to worship as equals; there is no priest or minister to lead the worship. In formal settings such as the Nineteen Day Feast (see below), a programme of readings, prayers and music is chosen by the Local Spiritual Assembly or by a committee or individual on the Assembly's behalf; community members may be asked ahead of time to act as readers. On less formal occasions those present may choose their own favourite passages and prayers to read.

Of course, prayer, reading and meditation by themselves are not enough. Bahá'ís have, too, to 'live the life', to strive to make Bahá'u'lláh's teachings a reality in their daily lives: to be loving, to build unity, to be trustworthy, to free themselves of prejudice, to accept the equality of women and men, to be of service to their fellow human beings, and so on. By embracing the Word of God, by tasting its sweetness, by opening their hearts to God in prayer and by responding in service, Bahá'ís develop a living relationship with Bahá'u'lláh.

One arena for spiritual growth is a practice known as 'Bahá'í consultation', which is used in Bahá'í Assemblies, in families and amongst friends, to arrive at an illumination of truth and to make decisions better than any individual could make alone. The first thing is to pray together. Bahá'ís in consultation then set out the facts as far as they understand them and express their

'Abdu'l-Baha, eldest son of Baha'u'llah. He was the Head of the Baha'i community from 1892 to 1921 and visited the West twice, in 1911 and 1912-13. For Baha'is he is the perfect example of how to live a Baha'i life.

views and opinions frankly but courteously, and from the clash of differing opinions, a spark of truth emerges. Bahá'ís strive to arrive at consensus; if, in formal consultation, consensus cannot be reached the matter is decided by a vote. The final part of consultation is the one that requires the greatest degree of personal maturity and detachment: each Bahá'í, whether or not she or he voted for the decision, is committed to carrying out the decision. Without this last step, it is impossible to know whether the decision was a good one or not.

But the Bahá'í life is not all hard work. Periodically local communities gather for the Nineteen Day Feast. The Feasts are (or should be) joyous gatherings where children, youth and men and women of all ages celebrate God's praise, consult about the affairs of the community and break bread together. This is the heart of our community life and is the main point of contact between the community and the Assembly. The life of the community flows through this gathering. The local Assembly reports on its decisions and shares its hopes and concerns. There may be a letter from the National Spiritual Assembly or even from the Universal House of Justice. The community makes recommendations to the Local Assembly and the Bahá'ís deepen the fellowship that binds them together. It is during the Feast that community members become ever more strongly aware of the connections between the local, national and international levels of the community, connections through which love and information flow in all directions. The capacity of the Universal House of Justice to do its work depends vitally on the energy of individual Bahá'ís and their local communities all over the world.

Throughout the year Bahá'ís mark a number of Holy Days, including nine on which they refrain from work. These days commemorate or celebrate major events in Bahá'í history. The most important of these is the twelve-day festival of *Ridván* or 'paradise', which celebrates Bahá'u'lláh's announcement that he was the one foretold by the Báb, the Manifestation of God.

Small communities meet in Bahá'í homes. Larger communities may have a Bahá'í Centre for their gatherings. On each continent there is a House of Worship, a nine-sided building whose Arabic name means 'Dawning Place of the Praise of God'. These houses of worship are gifts from the Bahá'í community to the peoples of the world; all are welcome of whatever faith or none; the only words heard during the services in these buildings are from the world's scriptures, read by individuals or sung by a *cappella* choir.

And who pays for all this? The Bahá'ís and only the Bahá'ís, who consider it a privilege to be able to contribute to the Bahá'í Fund. Donations are neither solicited nor accepted from those who are not Bahá'ís. The needs of the Bahá'í funds are made known to the Bahá'ís, but it is up to each individual to determine whether or not to contribute and, if so, how much.

Bahá'ís are much engaged in the life of the wider community: charitable work, involvement in Agenda 21, human rights, women's organizations, work for moral development and racial equality, amongst other issues. They work for a deep-rooted and lasting peace in the world and Bahá'ís from the UK have attended all the major UN summits and conferences from the 1992 Earth Summit in Rio forward. The Bahá'í International Community has consultative status with ECOSOC, the UN's Economic and Social Council.

Making Contact

Christians may well encounter Bahá'ís in various forums and organizations of social change or in local interfaith groups. Feel free to introduce yourself and ask questions. Bahá'ís are inclusive people and love to build friendships; they will be happy to answer your questions or to point you in the direction of someone else who can do so. And they will be happy to suggest a book with more information. Many Bahá'í individuals and communities hold regular 'firesides', hospitable and informal discussion meetings, as well as prayer meetings, social gatherings and study meetings to which all are welcome. If you don't get invited, try inviting yourself! However, you should be aware that the Nineteen Day Feast is for Bahá'ís only.

Bahá'u'lláh challenges everyone, whether Bahá'í or not, to know through their own knowledge and not through the knowledge of their neighbour, to search out the reality of things for themselves and not rely on hearsay or tradition. Bahá'ís love to ask questions and to delve into the texts and are always happy when others would like to read the Bahá'í scriptures and the wealth of secondary literature that is available.

Notes

The writings below can be obtained from the Baha'i Publishing Trust (see p. 71)
1. *Epistle to the Son of the Wolf*, pp. 20–21.
2. *Gleanings from the Writings of Bahá'u'lláh*, p. 99.
3. Bahá'u'lláh, *Kitáb-i-Aqdas*, parag. 19.
4. Bahá'u'lláh, *Kitáb-i-Aqdas*, parag. 182.
5. Bahá'u'lláh, *Kitáb-i-Íqán*, parag. 192.
6. *Gleanings from the Writings of Bahá'u'lláh*, parag. CXVII.
7. *Gleanings from the Writings of Bahá'u'lláh*, para. XCIII.
8. *Epistle to the Son of the Wolf*, p. 14.
9. *Epistle to the Son of the Wolf*, p. 12.

Questions for discussion

1. How do you respond to Bahá'u'lláh's teaching that God's truth is revealed progressively to humankind and always will be?

2. How do Bahá'u'lláh's teachings about the nature of the Manifestations of God compare with Christian belief about the nature of Jesus? How far can the Christian and Bahá'í positions be reconciled?

3. One of the dangers that besets people of faith is the belief that they are right and others are wrong. Bahá'u'lláh enjoins all of us to continue to investigate the truth and reality of all things. How do you respond to the challenges involved in finding out about other faiths?

4. Bahá'ís, like Christians, understand worship and the life of service to be two sides of a single coin. What similarities do you find between Christian and Bahá'í approaches to worship and service? What differences do you think there are?

The Bahá'í House of Worship in Delhi, India.

Chapter Two

The Buddhists: a view and a way

Elizabeth J Harris

The Beginnings

The image of the Buddha seated in meditation, hands resting on his lap, back erect, eyes downcast is one of the world's most well-known religious symbols. It breathes tranquillity and has inspired millions for over two centuries. Now, it is speaking to many in the West.

Buddhism is one of Britain's fastest growing religions. There are few towns which do not boast at least a Buddhist meditation house-group and there is hardly a city without a Buddhist centre of some kind, frequented both by those born Buddhist, new converts and others attracted by Buddhism's meditation techniques.

To the outsider, the external faces of Buddhism in Britain can seem bewilderingly diverse. This is not surprising since, during the twentieth century, Britain received Buddhism in almost all of its forms - something unique in the history of Buddhism. Buddhism began, in this era of time, in India in the fifth or sixth century BCE.[1] Then, it spread. From the beginning, it was a missionary religion. It travelled south to Sri Lanka, Thailand, Burma, and Cambodia and also north along trade routes to Pakistan, Afghanistan, China, Korea, Japan and Vietnam. Eventually, it crossed the Himalayas to Tibet. Everywhere it went, it adapted, drawing into itself aspects of the cultures it met.

Now, there are three major groupings within Buddhism, all of which have their roots in India: Theravada Buddhism found in the countries Buddhism reached as it went south; Mahayana Buddhism found in the areas reached when it went north and east and Vajrayana, the Buddhism of Tibet, which many see as a form of Mahayana. The groupings are not watertight, even in Asia. And in the West, new patterns are emerging as Buddhism adapts to yet another context.

It was in the nineteenth century, as a consequence of empire, that information about Buddhism that was more than fictitious, false or fantastic entered Britain. The Theravada tradition was the first to gain followers. Britain had imperial control over Burma and Sri Lanka (Ceylon) and therefore information flowed more readily from these countries than from Mahayana areas. The first formal Buddhist mission to Britain was in 1908, from Burma, led by a British convert living in Rangoon. Later in the twentieth century, Zen Buddhism, a Mahayana tradition from Japan, arrived as teachers such as D.T. Suzuki (1870-1966) travelled to America and Europe. Then, after China's invasion of Tibet in the 1950s, Buddhist teachers from different Tibetan schools travelled west. Scotland now boasts the largest Tibetan Buddhist Centre in the whole of Europe, Samye Ling. Centres were also established in Britain for people originally from countries such as Thailand, Sri Lanka and Vietnam. In addition, movements have begun which do not align themselves with a specific school, for example the Friends of the Western Buddhist Order (FWBO) which has sought to create a 'Western' Buddhism free from what are seen as cultural accretions from Asia. In the present, there are also centres which seek to create an ecumenical meeting point for Buddhists from all schools, placing more emphasis on free inquiry than adherence to a particular lineage.

An Underlying Unity

In the face of this diversity, to describe what Buddhists believe and practice is fraught with difficulty. Yet, there is an underlying unity, a common pool of attitudes and concerns within all Buddhist groupings which centres around what Buddhists call the three jewels: the Buddha, the Dharma or what the Buddha taught and the Sangha, the community of followers. To look at each in turn is one way of entering Buddhism.

The Buddha

The word *budh* or *buddhi* means wisdom, enlightenment or awakening. A Buddha is one who has awoken to truth, one who has seen into the nature of human life. Buddhists believe that there have been numerous Buddhas in the past. Each saw the truth and preached it out of compassion for the world. Within this era, the person recognized by all Buddhists as a Buddha is Siddhartha Gautama. There is no doubt that he was a historical figure but scholars dispute his dates. The traditional view that he lived in the sixth century BCE is now being replaced by a later dating of the fifth century BCE.

The words 'Almighty God' or 'Creator God' are never used to describe Gautama. In fact, the concept of a creator God does not feature in Buddhism. A Buddha is a human who, as a result of countless preparatory lives of self-sacrifice and effort, reaches a state of perfect wisdom and perfect compassion. One phrase used in Theravada Buddhism is *acchariya manussa* - wonderful, extraordinary man. Throughout Asia, Buddhists prostrate in front of Buddha images. They offer lights, incense and flowers. But they are not worshipping a god and certainly not an idol. They are showing reverence to an 'extraordinary man' and, especially in Mahayana Buddhism, to the cosmic concept of Buddhahood.

According to text and tradition, Siddhartha Gautama was born into an aristocratic ruling family in a republic in the north-east of India and spent his life in what is now Uttar Pradesh and Bihar. Biographies of his life were not written until several hundred years after his death and, by that time, embellishments had been added. In what are thought to be earlier texts there is only a hint here and a hint there. The traditional story goes something like this. After Siddhartha was born, sages predicted that he would be either a world renouncer and a Buddha or a world ruler. To prevent the former, his parents protected him from all intimations of pain, suffering and poverty. In his late adolescence, he married his cousin, Yasodhara. Eventually, a son was born to them. One day, however, he went out, accompanied only by his charioteer, and, for the first time, encountered suffering through seeing an old person, a sick person and a corpse. This was followed by the sight of a holy man who had renounced home and family.

This encounter with human pain threw Siddhartha into turmoil. Luxury and comfort no longer pleased. So, soon afterwards, he left his wife and son to become a 'wanderer', a searcher after religious truth, and there were many at this time in India. For six years, he searched and experimented. He practised meditation under two of the most renowned teachers of the day but left each, dissatisfied, having mastered all they could teach. He then joined a group of ascetics and ate so little that his body became skeleton-like. According to the Theravada texts, he reached the point when, touching his belly, his hand reached his backbone.

Realizing that self-punishment was not bringing him nearer his goal of gaining insight into the causes of suffering, the Buddha-to-be began to eat. Immediately, he was seen as a traitor by his ascetic companions. But it was only after rejecting asceticism, that he gained enlightenment, sitting in meditation under what is now called a Bodhi Tree near present-day Gaya, on the night of the Full Moon. He was thirty five years old. For the next forty five years, he taught in north-east India, gradually drawing around him an extensive following, his wife and son among them. These consisted both of those who stayed within their families as lay disciples and the men and eventually women who renounced home and family to become celibate monastics.

Theravada Buddhists look almost exclusively to Siddhartha Gautama. Mahayana Buddhists also revere him but see him as an embodiment of a cosmic principle of Buddhahood to which all humans can attain. For Mahayanists, all can become Buddhas and Buddhas can be as numerous as 'the sands on the river Ganges'.

The Dharma

The overriding existential issue for the Buddha was the existence of suffering. His pre-enlightenment search was not so much for metaphysical truth as for the answer to an empirical problem: why are we born to a life of anguish and pain? From what he eventually 'saw' flowed a liberative teaching which embraced ethics, social justice, political organization and gender equality, though most importantly transformation of the mind and heart. He was a person of dialogue who entered the philosophical discussion of his day with vigour and a willingness to talk with people from all social strata. He was not afraid to be critical of the caste system, elaborate religious ritual, animal sacrifice and political corruption. Yet, the call to which many responded by leaving their families to become 'monastics' was simple, 'Come, live the holy life and put an end to suffering.'

An End to Suffering

At the heart of the Buddha's answer to the question of suffering lay the law of cause and effect. Everything in the round of birth and rebirth is conditioned, he insisted. Nothing is random. Everything is interlinked through a complex web of cause and effect. He then pinpointed a cause of suffering and stressed that if this could be eradicated, the very law of cause and effect would mean that suffering could not arise.

The cause pinpointed by the Buddha was threefold - greed, hatred and delusion or ignorance. In the Tibetan Wheel of Life, one of the most popular pieces of Buddhist art, greed, hatred and delusion appear at the very centre, as animals circling around, catching each other's tail. All human ill flows from the three, according to Buddhism. To take delusion or ignorance first, the Buddha insisted that human existence was characterized by three things - impermanence, suffering or unsatisfactoriness, and no-self (the lack of anything unchanging in the human person). Ignorance was not seeing this. It was to assume that life contains the permanent, that youth remains, that possessions last. It was also to believe that there is an unchanging 'I' which needs to be protected, promoted.

The Buddha placed particular emphasis on the last. The terms 'I' and 'mine' are illusion, he taught; there is nothing in the human body or mind to which they correspond and clinging to them is one of the chief causes of suffering. That there are human persons he did not deny nor that there was continuity after death. What was denied was that there is an unchanging essence within the human body that is separate from the rest of the world and therefore has to be defended from it, an unchanging essence that is unaffected by the dynamics of change and the law of cause and effect that governs everything else around us. 'That is not how the body and mind work,' the Buddha insisted. Moving from selfishness to self-lessness was, therefore, necessary. As for greed and hatred, Buddhism sees them as almost inseparable from the ignorance which feeds them. When the self is clung to, when the impermanent is thought to be permanent, humans are thrown back and forth between longing and repulsion, attraction and aversion. Ignorance, greed and hatred reinforce each other in an endless cycle unless the inner dynamic can be seen and rooted out.

This teaching is sometimes reduced to the Four Noble Truths. The first is the noble truth of suffering - that life has, at its heart, something which is unsatisfactory, disjointed, painful. The second is the noble truth of arising - that this unsatisfactoriness is caused by selfish craving. Then comes the noble truth of cessation - that suffering can be eradicated if this craving is rooted out i.e. by virtue of the law of cause and effect. The last is the noble truth of the path to the cessation of suffering - the Eightfold Path which consists of right understanding, right thought, right speech, right action, right livelihood, right effort, right mindfulness, right concentration.

The Way out of Suffering

The Buddha's message was, in effect, this: 'the way you see the world is false; the way you act within the world is based on illusion; Change! Turn round! Start on the path which will lead to freedom from suffering.' It was an activist message. Buddhists are happier if Buddhism is presented as a way of life rather than a system of beliefs. Confidence (akin to faith) that the teaching of the Buddha is true is usually seen as the first step and devotion to the memory of the Buddha is important to many but then it is all action, all practice. One verse that sums up for many Buddhists the heart of their faith is:

> The avoidance of all evil; the undertaking of good; the cleansing of one's mind; this is the teaching of the awakened ones.[2]

Morality

Morality is the essential bedrock of all Buddhist practice. It lies at the heart of the Eightfold Path. In Theravada Buddhist countries, no Buddhist ceremony is complete without all present 'taking' what are known as the five precepts, which involves voluntarily abstaining from: harming living beings; taking what is not given; false speech; sexual misconduct and using anything that will damage the mind, for example alcohol or drugs. Abstaining from harming self and harming others lies at the heart of them. Developing the positive qualities of loving kindness, generosity and compassion goes hand in hand with them. On this foundation everything else rests.

Meditation

Rooting out greed, hatred and delusion, all Buddhists would agree, involves more than moral living. It demands changing the heart and mind at a very deep level through mental culture. This is where meditation comes in. It is represented in the Eightfold Path as right mindfulness and right concentration. It is a discipline which nurtures tranquillity, self-knowledge and insight. The different schools of Buddhism have developed different techniques. One major distinction drawn by many Buddhists is between tranquillity meditation and insight meditation. The former involves concentrating on an object, for example the breath, in order to gain the kind of one-pointedness of mind that leads to calm and, for advanced meditators, to what are called meditative absorptions or higher states of consciousness. Insight meditation, on the other hand, involves developing 'mindfulness' through 'bare attention' to all that is happening in the mind and heart so that insight can be gained into how one's own mind and heart work, namely how greed and hatred arise and pass, how the mind is conditioned to feel attraction and aversion and ultimately how

A nun in the Tibetan tradition, photographed at Angkor Wat.

everything is characterised by impermanence and no-self, or emptiness as many Mahayana Buddhists would put it.

Another very popular form of meditation is meditation on loving kindness (*metta* in Pali). This involves radiating loving kindness into the cosmos through visualizing certain individuals or groups of people and surrounding them with the warmth of this quality. The first step is often to surround oneself with loving kindness and then, from oneself, to move outwards - to family, to teachers, to friends and neighbours, to people in need or places of war, and, most significantly, to those one does not like. For many Buddhists this is a daily practice.

The Goal

Buddhists believe in continuity after death but the goal of religious practice is not focussed on an after-death state. In fact, death is believed to lead to rebirth after rebirth, in an endless and horrific cycle, if greed, hatred and delusion are not destroyed. The goal of Buddhism is to be released from this cycle. All Buddhist schools speak with joy and wonder at the liberation that comes when greed, hatred and ignorance are no more. Called *nirvana* (Sanskrit) or *nibbana* (Pali), the texts describe it as the highest happiness, the highest bliss, the highest truth. Greed and hatred are no more. Clinging to self and the 'I' has evaporated. Compassion and wisdom, the two poles of enlightenment, have arisen instead. Mahayana Buddhists call this realizing one's Buddha-nature. Some Buddhists see this happening to them many lives into the future; others insist it could happen in this very life. As to what happens after death to the one who is enlightened or awakened, the texts imply that human language simply cannot describe it. But it is certainly not annihilation.

The Sangha

Sangha means community or congregation. Buddhism was born in community. Those who left their home and family to follow the Buddha as renunciants entered a community and gradually a rule of discipline evolved, the aim of which was to nurture positive, egalitarian relationships among its members. From the beginning, this 'monastic' Sangha was dependent on the laity for food and clothing and the laity on this Sangha for teaching and encouragement. Therefore, the Theravada texts speak of a fourfold community: lay women, lay men, women renunciants and male renunciants.

In many Asian countries today, however, the term Sangha has come to denote only those who are ordained as monks and, where women are still able to gain higher ordination, nuns. For lay people, the third refuge is those who wear robes. In fact, the robe worn by the Buddhist renunciant has come to be seen almost as the representative of the Buddha on earth. Lay people in Asia will still bow down to a Buddhist monk in the same way as they prostrate before a Buddha image.

Especially in the West, however, the term Sangha is increasingly being seen as denoting the whole community of practitioners. For groups such as the Western Buddhist Order, this has to be, since it has rejected the lay/ordained distinction as irrelevant for the West. Whichever interpretation is used, the word gives voice to the importance within Buddhism both of community and of teaching. Although there are Buddhists who follow a solitary life of meditation practice - ancient caves used for this can be found all over Asia - great stress is placed on the importance of good friends and a reliable teacher for anyone attempting to follow the Buddhist path.

An offering is made to a Buddhist nun at an international conference for Buddhist women in Cambodia.

Stereotypes Contested

Christians have accused Buddhism in the past of being both nihilistic and exclusively concerned with withdrawal from society. Both are misrepresentations. My words about the positive qualities of *nirvana* should dispel the first. The second accusation can be contested by pointing to the many places in the world where Buddhists are involved in peace-making, human rights work, rural development and conflict resolution. Initiatives such as the International Network of Engaged Buddhists, started by a group of people which included Sulak Sivaraksa from Thailand and Thich Nhat Hanh from Vietnam, stress that personal transformation and social transformation must go together. In the West, Buddhists are involved with issues as various as protection of the environment, soup-kitchens in Moscow, education projects in India and self-help groups for the psychologically wounded. Buddhism does speak about non-attachment but it is non-attachment to all those things that cause havoc in society, such as greed, hatred, craving and selfishness, not detachment from concern for human life.

Where Faiths Touch

At one level, Buddhism and Christianity can seem poles apart, especially on the question of divinity. Yet, the touching points between them are numerous and this is being recognized by both Christians and Buddhists. Inter-monastic dialogue, particularly between Zen monks in Japan and western Christian monks has been happening for several decades.[3] Both the Dalai Lama and Thich Nhat Hanh have spoken or written on Buddhist- Christian relationships.[4] There are Buddhist centres that host Christian-Buddhist meditation retreats lead jointly by a Buddhist and a Christian. Associations for Buddhist-Christian Studies exist in several parts of the world.[5]

Notes

1. Many books give the dates of the Buddha as about 566-486 BCE. However, recent scholars by re-assessing the evidence think that the dates are more likely to have been 480-400 BCE.
2. *Dhammapada*, verse 183, translation taken from *The Word of the Doctrine*, Translated by K. R. Norman, Oxford, Pali Text Society, 1997, p. 28. The Dhammapada is a text which is found, in differing forms, within several schools of Buddhism. This translation is taken from the text as it appears in the Theravada Canon. It is a much loved collection of proverb-like verses which capture major themes in Buddhist practice.
3. See, for example: Eds. Donald W. Mitchell and James Wiseman, O.S.B., *The Gethsemani Encounter: A Dialogue on the Spiritual Life by Buddhist and Christian Monastics,* New York and London, Continuum, 1999
4. For example, Thich Nhat Hanh, *Living Buddha, Living Christ,* London, Rider, 1995 and *Going Home: Jesus and Buddha as Brothers*, London, Rider, 1999; Ed. Robert Kiely, *The Good Heart: His Holiness the Dalai Lama explores the heart of Christianity - and of humanity*, Rider, 1996. See also: Eds. Rita M. Gross and Terry Muck, *Buddhists Talk about Jesus, Christians talk about the Buddha*, London and New York, Continuum, 2000.
5. The oldest association is the Society of Buddhist-Christian Studies in America, which grew out of a Buddhist-Christian conference in 1987 held in Berkeley. They produce an annual journal, *Buddhist-Christian Studies*, and organize periodic conferences. The European Network of Buddhist-Christian Studies was formed in the 1990s.

Chapter Three

Hindu Faith and Tradition

Eric Lott

I have agreed to an impossible task! For there are so many different ways of being Hindu, even if in this country the religious and cultural life of Hindu people tends to be more uniform. But I shall try, within the limits of this article, to do some justice to the immense diversity within Hindu faith and tradition. People speak about 'the unchanging East'. Some features do remain little touched. But the religion and culture of Hindu people has for several millennia been in a dynamic process of change and interaction. Modernity now makes its impact. I shall focus on nine features of the Hindu tradition which I see as essential.

A Strong Sense of the Sacred

Almost everywhere you turn in India there are signs of the Sacred and a great forest of symbolism. There is a strong belief that trans-human powers impinge upon our life at every turn, both for good and for ill. Throughout the year, therefore, there are sacred festivals - Navratri ('Nine Nights'), Divali ('Row of Lights') being only two. At Divali, for example, Lakshmi, the Goddess of good fortune, is given importance, and merchants begin their accounting afresh at that time. It is mostly through the main festivals that more corporate religious and social celebration takes place, though in this country temples make *Arati*, the fire-waving before the shrines, a kind of daily service.

Every critical point in life's progress too is marked by sacred action - naming, cradle-placing, hair-cutting, learning the first letter, initiation into the sacred community and its knowledge, marriage, pregnancy, birth, travel, return, death, anniversary of death, etc.

Within this celebrating of the Sacred at every point in life the frequent threat of evil powers is also felt. The prayer of Jesus, 'Deliver us from evil', expresses a very basic concern in Hinduism. Unless proper measures are taken, all manner of evil and misfortune can afflict the unwary. At the popular level there will be wearing of charms and amulets, consulting astrologers and clairvoyants, perhaps even blood-sacrifice; all intended to ward off danger and the Evil-eye. But overcoming evil is not merely a matter of appeasing evil powers or performing magical acts: it is more importantly overcome in Hinduism by proper attunement with God and the power of Good.

The Power of Sacred Places

India is a land of countless temples and shrines. Some attract huge numbers of pilgrims (and staggering amounts of income by way of offering). In all temples it is the image in which the Sacred Power is especially embodied and although every devout home will also have its household shrine and chosen images, pilgrimage to the sacred places will feature high on the agenda of Hindu faith. Setting out on pilgrimage may first call for rigorous self-preparation e.g. for devotees of Ayyappa, 40 days of nightly praise-singing, careful fasting and abstaining from sex, walking barefoot and wearing black cotton; then the journey to and walking up the long forest-hill to the shrine of Ayyappa in Kerala. This pilgrimage, made by many thousands each year, is an all-male affair, to the irritation of some women Hindus.

There is no such gender-bar in the equally popular journey to visit Murugun - a local deity drawn into the family of the 'Great God' Siva - on Palni Hill in Tamilnad. In early Spring each year great crowds of rural people pour towards Palni from as far as a hundred miles away, wearing saffron and walking barefoot night and day. Sharing the food they carry with them, strong social bonding takes place as they journey. Imagine the intense corporate emotion as the sacred hill comes into view and together they climb the steps leading up to *darsan*, their 'vision' of the God who is the focus of their devotion. Part of any pilgrimage will also involve ritual bathing in a sacred pool or river, making a vow, procession (clockwise) around the sacred shrine, some form of offering, including coconut, fruit, money, perhaps one's hair, and receiving back from the priest sacred *prasadam* (symbolic food for God).

Peace to the Whole Earth as Sacred Mother

While a typical Hindu world view finds many special focal points for the Sacred, in general the whole earth is seen as a sacred Mother. The orthodox Hindu asks for forgiveness even for stepping onto Earth when rising from bed in the morning. Another long Earth-prayer in the ancient Vedas pleads that in our ploughing and mining of earth, we may not 'pierce to your vital heart'. Other prayers are for the blessing of peace on all the elements. And there is prominence given to a number of birds and animals as the 'bearers' of the Sacred: Garuda the Eagle bears Vishnu; the Bull bears Siva; the Swan bears Sarasvati, goddess of the arts and music. Vishnu is embodied as Fish, Tortoise, Boar, Man-lion. And the Cow, 'giver of plenty', is of course the most potent symbol of the Sacred in animal life. Tribal culture in India too in general affirms close relationship with nature, or with focal points of the Sacred in nature.

This makes all the more surprising - to some Hindus too - the recent acclaim by the majority of Indians of their nuclear explosions as a proud emergence of a 'Hindu bomb'. The fact is, though, that there has always been a violent as well as a peaceful side of Hindu tradition. Mahatma Gandhi, with his message of non-violent protest and change, is not the only representative of twentieth century Hindu social attitude. Hinduism has never been the totally tolerant religion so often claimed. Even so, there is no doubting the strong peace-strand in its tradition; there is much that is eco-friendly, seeking participation in earth's life, rather than the aggressive dominance, that has all too often typified western Christendom.

The Importance of Sacred Story

Every temple and place of pilgrimage has its 'ancient story', aiming to account for its sacral 'greatness'. These stories describe, in mythic style, how the God worshipped there first 'visited' and blessed the place with his or her presence and power. In fact, such sacred stories form a large part of Hindu tradition. Hindu faith is transmitted from generation to generation largely in story form. Festivals often culminate in the public re-telling of such stories - perhaps as song recitals, as 'stories with a drum', or as full-blown dramatic presentations (about Rama and Sita for example), or as dance-dramas, of which a favourite is the 'playfulness' and dancing of the flute-playing cow-herd Krishna with the milkmaids. Any of these story-performances may last for several hours, well into the night.

Sacred Books

These are formally divided into (a) those directly 'heard' (i.e. the 'eternal Sound' heard by the ancients, said to have their own intrinsic authority, not having been composed by anyone, not even God); and (b) those 'remembered', which properly speaking have less revelatory authority.

Siva and his wife Parvati dancing as part of the creative process.

Linked to the four Vedas are the 'secret' writings that are seen as so revelatory in the later metaphysical theology called Vedanta.

Many scriptures are made up largely of the age-old stories I noted above. This is especially so with the Puranas ('ancient') and Epics, which are the Ramayana (story of the ideal king Rama) and Maha-bharata (the story of the great war within the family of Bharata, legendary patriarch of India; this huge book includes that immensely popular 'Gospel of Hinduism', the Bhagavad-Gita, or Song of the Lord'). Perhaps the most significant Purana is the Bhagavata, featuring the flute-playing, dancing Krishna, loved by countless devotees who have seen in his love-play the story of their own soul's journey to blissful union with God. The Hare Krishna movement, in which so many westerners have been caught up, takes this scripture as their special source of spiritual insight. Other sects have taken other writings, sometimes quite obscure and esoteric, as their revelatory source.

Special Sects and the 'Love-Drowned'

Of the hundreds of different sub-sects within Hinduism, three stand out, grouped around the Gods Vishnu and Siva, and the Goddess sometimes called Sakti, or 'Power'. Many Hindus do not relate to any particular sect; yet probably the most powerful devotional writing, as well as the most outstanding systematic theology, has sprung up within such special devotional groupings. For example, in the period from the fifth to ninth centuries CE, 12 ecstatic poets called the 'Drowned Ones' (i.e. drowned in divine love) poured out their passion for Vishnu, focussed in his Krishna-embodied form. Their poems are in some ways similar in style and tone to the Jesus-centred evangelical outpouring of Charles Wesley. Some of the twelve were of lowly, polluted birth in Hindu terms; one was a woman. And about the same time passionate devotees of Siva were also singing his praises in similar style. In both sects among the Tamil people even today these love-songs still inspire great devotion.

In both sects too passionate poetry was the inspiration, from the eleventh century onwards, for a rich **theology of devotion** (bhakti) in which relationship with God, based on divine love, was ultimate. The nature of God's grace was fiercely debated though. Did it function as the cat, which lifts up her helpless kitten, or like the monkey, where the young one has to cling on to its caring mother?

It is usually said that the highest Hindu aspiration is to be set free (mukti, moksha) from bondage to karma's unending cycle of birth and rebirth, to be free from all relational life. In this wide-spread religion of God-love, though, there is no higher life-goal than to be devoted to God, bound in a love-relationship for eternity. That is claimed as the desired moksha.

God and Belief-Systems

To the outsider, Hindu religion often looks like polytheism - faith in many separate gods, each with an eternally distinct role. Ask almost any devout Hindu, though, and you will be told there is in reality only one God. Usually it is said that the one god of all has to be manifest in different ways in order to fit the different needs of people - needs that are geographic, spiritual, functional. A similar account is given of image-worship. In reality the God to be worshipped is beyond all 'name and form', even if God graciously empowers an image so as to be accessible to devotees.

I have mentioned the theology which sprang out of the poetry of the 'love-drowned'. Belief-systems within Hindu religion range much wider than that of course. Vedanta is the most

Krishna, the flute-playing lover of the milk girls.

serious form of Hindu reflection on faith. It is divided into six distinctive ways of thinking about the nature of God (usually called Brahman, or the Supreme Self). The obvious questions they engage with are: What is the essential nature of God? How does this Supreme Person, the Source and inmost Life of all, relate to that 'all'? Is the world real or ultimately illusory? What does it mean to say creation is the playfulness of God? How do souls attain their freedom from the bondage that ensnares them?

Two fundamentally opposed viewpoints stand out. Though a number of recent interpreters deny any real contradiction, the original exponents were fiercely clear about their differences. There is a transcendentalism which says that created life, looked at from the standpoint of ultimate truth, ultimate oneness, is illusory. The other theology says that this creative process is ultimately real, just as the personal being of the God from whom creation derives is real. For the whole universe is the 'inseparably related body' of God, its inmost Self, and therefore is utterly dependent upon the creative power, life and love of that God.

Embodiments of God on Earth

The universe as God's body may be significant theologically; but in popular experience other divine embodiments are more potent. I have already touched briefly on the image-embodiments of temples. Lying behind these is the belief that God comes to earth at times of crisis to rescue those in need, usually in response to their cry of faith. There are ten main Avatars or Descents of God, ranging from the primal Fish to Krishna and even to the 'One who is to come'. Interpretation of these Avatars is varied. For some they are only 'manifestations', perhaps merely appearing 'as though' in bodily form; others insist that God in each Avatar takes a real body, though untouched by any impurity.

It is the two Avatars Rama and (as we saw) Krishna who have inspired the most intense adoration, expressed in attractive regional languages rather than priestly Sanskrit. The passionate movements surrounding them were more inclusive than any other in Hinduism. As Krishna puts it in the Bhagavad Gita:

> Whoever takes me as refuge, even though of lowly birth,
> Even women and polluted workers, will walk the highest way.

Even spiritual Guides and those thought able to lift people to a new level of insight - Gurus, Swamijis and suchlike - may be seen as Avatars of God. God is believed to touch human life through these charismatic figures. Of the prominent God-figures in our time one is Satya Sai Baba. Born in rural South India, his teachings are not very special - though he does claim to bring together the essence of all true religions. Yet this ability to attract followers from outside the Hindu fold is typical of many present-day Gurus. What makes the impression in the case of Sai Baba is the divine power he is believed to exude, leading to many claims of miracles, often when he is far distant from the person experiencing the strange happening.

Conforming to the Eternal Order of Things

Many Hindus affirm that to be 'Hindu' is not essentially to do with particular belief or 'religious' experience at all. It is rather to be part of a certain socio-cultural way of life and its ethos. It is to find one's place within the eternal dharma, the proper ordering of life - personal, social, cosmic. It was this *dharma*, threatened by evil-doers, that God came to re-establish through his Avatars, according to the Gita.

Basic to Hindu *dharma* is the social hierarchical system of caste. Hindu apologists interpret caste as mere difference of function, or as an inclusive way of giving place to the many different tribal groups gradually drawn into the Hindu fold. Yet, even within Indian society radical thinkers see the caste system as a major hindrance to social progress. It tends to create a communalist mind-set and belief in caste is locked into belief in the determining law of *karma*: what we are now (high-born and pure, or low-born and polluted) is the result of what we did in previous births, and what we shall become in future births will result from what we do now. It is easy to see why Dalits (the 'broken', 'oppressed', once called 'untouchables' and 'outcaste') find any such *dharmic/karmic* view of human society quite abhorrent. It is at this point that a Hindu view of life is most seriously challenged.

Chapter Four

The Jains – Looking Beyond Limitations

Michael Ipgrave

The name of Raichand Mehta is little remembered today, yet he was the spiritual mentor of one of the nineteenth century's greatest figures: Mohandas K Gandhi. It was from Raichand that Gandhi learnt the principle and practice of non-violence which he was to use so powerfully in the struggle for India's freedom. Raichand, a jeweller by trade, was a devout member of the Jain community and his influence on Gandhi is typical of the part Jainism has played throughout the centuries in India.

The Jains are a small community, numbering only around eight million worldwide (of whom 50,000 are in Britain), yet their ideas and their example have had an influence out of all proportion to their numbers.

The example of Raichand Mehta is a good starting-point for understanding who the Jains are, what they believe and what way of living they commend.

Gandhi described his friend in these words: 'He was one who had gone beyond all religious limitations and had succeeded in completely identifying himself with every living creature. He was free from contradiction between speech and behaviour'. We can pick out five significant points from this:-

❖ Most importantly, the message Raichand passed on to Gandhi was that of non-violence. Under the name of '*ahimsa*', this has always been central to Jainism.

❖ Gandhi described him as "completely identifying himself with every living creature". Jain spirituality shows an intense feeling of kinship with other species.

❖ Gandhi's comment that Raichand was one who went 'beyond all religious limitations' points to the Jain philosophy of '*anekantavada*' or 'plural thinking'.

❖ The comment that Raichand's speech and behaviour perfectly mirrored one another points to the importance in Jainism of codes of ethics.

❖ Finally, Raichand was typical of his community in combining spirituality with a successful career as a jeweller. The Jains are a generally prosperous and confident community, predominantly involved in business.

Ahimsa

Ahimsa is literally a negative: 'not' ('a') violence ('himsa'). In practice, it is a positive commitment to cause no harm to any other living being. This ideal was proclaimed by Mahavira, whom Jains revere as the 24th and last of the 'Tirthankaras' or great teachers of their faith, in sixth century BCE India. Like his contemporary the Buddha, Mahavira promised a way of liberation for the soul open to all, irrespective of caste, social status or gender (though the last point was to be as disputed in subsequent Jainism as in Buddhism).

This way, of *ahimsa*, was a protest against the casual cruelty he saw all around him: 'All

Carvings in marble on the front of the Jain temple in Leicester.

breathing, existing, living, sentient creatures should not be slain, nor treated with violence, nor abused, nor tormented, nor driven away. This is the pure, unchangeable, eternal law.' (*Acaranga-sutra* 1.4.1) A common Jain slogan declares '*ahimsa paramo dharmah*', 'non-violence is the highest religious duty'. *Ahimsa* has remained central to Jainism since Mahavira's time but there are different ways of applying it in daily life.

On one hand, in every generation a small number of men and women enter upon the ascetic way. They completely renounce possessions, comfort and stability to become homeless wanderers, reliant on alms for survival. *Ahimsa* for Jain monks and nuns is a code of conduct regulating every detail of existence. Walking along the road, they sweep the ground before them so as not to crush any small insects. They do not light fires, dig or plough the ground. They drink only boiled or filtered water, and so on.

Most Jain men and women, though, live their lives in the complexities of human society. They belong to families, they earn their own living and they are surrounded by possessions. So for them the strict requirements of *ahimsa* have been modified. Even so, lay Jains too, will seek to lead as non-violent a life as possible. For a short period every day (usually 48 minutes) they may take upon themselves the vows of the monastic life. They generally choose professions which involve as little damage as possible to other beings. All practising Jains are vegetarians and the devout will not eat root crops, which are believed to have in them more 'life' than other vegetables.

Kinship and karma

An intense sense of kinship with other organisms underpins the practice of *ahimsa*. Jainism teaches that central to every living being is its indestructible soul (*jiva*), which passes through endless cycles of life, death and rebirth. In his influential book 'The Self-Realisation' (*Atma-Siddhi*), Raichand Mehta described the heart of Jain meditation as a coming to awareness of the reality of soul. At the end of each lifetime, the soul attaches to a different body, its choice governed by the law of karma. This law states that bad deeds weigh down the soul, leading to rebirth in a lower form of existence, while good deeds open the possibility of a higher grade of life for the soul. The operation of karma in Jainism is very complex, as in every existence there are not only future effects being generated in the present but also the legacy of previous existences.

However, one simple consequence of this sophisticated philosophy is the belief that other life forms – animals, plants, microscopic organisms, spiritual beings – are very close to humans. All are basically souls attached to bodies and it is quite possible that they may be our physical relatives through previous lives. This sense of the interdependence of all souls ('*parasparopagraho jivanam*') informs Jain attitudes to ecological issues. Jains in India have been pioneers in environmental protection. The Jain community is also generous in providing medical care for animals, most famously a large hospital for birds just opposite Red Fort in the heart of Delhi.

Plural thinking

As *ahimsa* is central to the Jain way of living, central to Jain thinking is the principle of '*anekantavada*', a cumbersome word which literally translates as 'non-one-sided-ness'. This is the recognition that a total understanding of any situation can only be obtained by combining viewpoints from a number of different perspectives. Partial theories are bound to be limited; to insist on one view to the exclusion of others is foolish and can lead to unnecessary conflict.

The Jains illustrate this point by a story well known in other traditions also – that of five blind men attempting to describe an elephant. Grasping the tail, one insists that it is a rope. Another, holding the trunk, denies this, assuring the other that it is a tree. A third, standing next to the elephant's leg, interprets it as a pillar. The other two, feeling the beast's ear and side, opt for a fan and a wall respectively. So tenacious are the five blind men in their partial theories that they soon fall to blows and it is only the intervention of a sage able to reconcile their differences that brings peace. The message of the parable is clear and contemporary Jains believe that it shows a particular contribution that they have to offer to our multi-faith and pluralistic world.

They are ready to welcome a variety of different viewpoints as being all partial expressions of different aspects of ultimate truth. So Jains are often very active in the cause of inter-faith understanding and they generally disown any interest in converting people from other religions to membership of the Jain community. However, such plurality in thinking does not mean that the Jains have no particular religious identity of their own.

While heavily influenced by the predominant Hindu milieu in which they have lived for millennia, the Jains have a distinctive and continuing tradition of worship and spirituality, with a rich heritage of art, architecture and literature. This developed over the centuries in India and it is there that one must go to see such wonders as the hilltop temple-city of Satrunjaya in Rajasthan, the colossal 60ft image of Bahubali standing in meditation at Sravana Belgola in Karnataka or the fabulously intricate carvings of the temples at Dilwara on Mount Abu, also in Rajasthan.

For those unable to travel to India, Leicester provides a good sampler of the glories of Jain art and architecture. The Jain centre on Oxford Street is an oasis of peace beside the city's busy inner ring road. Richly sculpted sandstone columns cluster together like a stone forest around the serene white marble figures of the Tirthankaras sitting in meditation. Here the community gathers for the great festivals and fasts of the Jain year, and here a handful of Jains come day by day to offer 'arati'. Circling a tray of ghee-lamps, they sing hymns praising the accomplishments of the Tirthankaras, those who have passed from this world's cycle of birth, death and rebirth to reach the unsurpassed bliss of that other world where the soul is finally set free.

Conquering the self

As they sing their devotional hymns, the Jains remember that it was through the unrelenting pursuit of a rigorously ethical life that the Tirthankaras achieved liberation. Equally, it is through living an ethical life that their devotees can hope to advance on the same path. Indeed, the very word 'Jain' (*Jaina*) denotes a follower of the Jina. The word 'Jina' (another title for Tirthankara) means the 'one who has conquered himself or herself'. So, through the practice of a disciplined life, true Jains are to overcome their unruly passions to achieve purification of the soul. This constant dimension of ethical struggle is acknowledged in the common salutation with which Jains greet one another: '*Jai Jinendra*' – 'homage to the one who has overcome'.

In practice, Jains emphasise many of the values held in common by other faiths. The code of conduct for laity lists five vows: non-violence, truthfulness, non-stealing, chastity and non-acquisitiveness. These are not just external norms: Jainism insists strongly that violence can be mental as well as physical. The roots of the actions and attitudes which harm others lie within us, so we have a responsibility to uproot them from our souls.

This leads to an emphasis on mutual accountability which finds moving expression on the last day of Paryushana, the greatest festival of the Jain year. Gathering together in the temple, members of the community greet their fellow Jains with the words '*micchami dukkadam*', 'may the harm I have caused you come to nothing'. In particular, they seek out those they may have wronged in some way during the last twelve months. So they ask forgiveness at the end of one year that they may begin the new year renewed in the spirit of mutual co-operation and friendship.

Influence in business

Ethics in turn have shaped the Jain community's business success in two ways. The commitment to *ahimsa* meant that from the earliest times Jains avoided agriculture, as tilling the soil was held to involve violence to innumerable organisms. Consequently, they involved themselves in financial and commercial areas of life as merchants and traders.

At the same time, the Jains' rigorous code of ethics gave them a name for fairness and honesty which brought prosperity and their austere lifestyle led them to set aside for investment money which might otherwise have been devoted to conspicuous consumption. The net effect of all this has been to give the Jains, despite their minority status, a very influential position within the Indian economy. Indeed, some areas, such as diamond trading, are almost wholly in Jain hands.

Interesting parallels can be drawn here with the experience of those English Quaker families who likewise acquired economic pre-eminence as a result of their exclusion from other areas of life and their conscientious business practices.

Jainism today

It is their confident and entrepreneurial spirit which led many Jains to be part of the great movement of Gujarati people from west India, first to the countries of East Africa and then to Britain, North America and other parts of the West. It will be interesting indeed to see how over the years the diaspora Jain community responds to the challenges of this new situation. Many Jains feel that their ancient faith has much to say of relevance to the contemporary world – they have been addressing, for instance, issues of religious plurality, of responsible environmental stewardship and of animal welfare long before these were recognised as pressing in the West.

Like every religious community today, the Jains experience tensions among themselves. As well as the historical divisions between different sects, there are disagreements between traditionalists and modernisers. It will be interesting also to see how the Jains respond to those outside their community who wish to try the Jain way for themselves. There is among many Jains a deep-seated reluctance to seek or even to accept new members. This reluctance is one sign of the great difference in history between Jainism and Buddhism: while the two faiths grew from the same time and place and with similar messages, Buddhism spread through Asia while Jainism remained a purely Indian phenomenon.

Will this pattern repeat itself in our own context, as a western form of Buddhism continues to grow while Jainism remains ethnically limited to the Indian community? Or will the desire of some Jains to commend the resources of their faith to a wider public see them develop a pattern of Jain 'mission' through the sharing of deeply held ethical and philosophical values?

Christians in particular have reason to watch such developments with interest. There are, of course, enormous divergences between our two faiths, which should be the subject of well-informed and respectful debate – for example, to name just three crucial questions: What is the nature and destiny of the human individual? Is divine grace regulated by scientific law or by free personal choice? What is the value of unmerited suffering?

Nor is this simply a question of exchanging views. Jains and Christians also have much to learn from each other in the area of spirituality. For example, Christian faith stresses that salvation is the free gift of God's unmerited grace, and this is central to the Gospel. However, it is all too easy to slide from this insight into the dangerous position that we do not really need to make much of an effort in our spiritual life, since our future destiny is assured already. Christian tradition of course repeatedly warns against this view but we can also learn much from the seriousness of the discipline expected of those who follow the way of the Jinas. The regular practice of austerities, the emphasis on self-overcoming and the insistence that the soul cannot look outside its self for any excuses to justify laxity – all these aspects of the Jain way are deeply impressive when expressed in the lives of devout Jains, and Christians can learn new perspectives on their own faith (or re-learn old perspectives) from recognising and exploring their spiritual values.

On the other hand, the primary Christian value of *agape*-love can equally be an inspiration for Jains to interpret the principle of *ahimsa* in an outgoing and inclusive sense. The stress on attaining liberation of the soul is so strong in Jainism that there can be a danger of excessive individualism: it is my karma which must be removed, my purity which must be secured. Yet *ahimsa* in fact need not be restricted to the self in this way: indeed, the great teachers of Jainism emphasise that it should extend to benefit all living beings with whom we are kin. Perhaps the Christian understanding of love in action and the social concern to which that has given rise, can encourage Jains in extending to their fellow human beings in particular a deep compassion based on a spirituality of *ahimsa*. Indeed, in India today, Jain philanthropists are increasingly involved in supporting social welfare projects, as well as their more traditional animal and environmental care schemes.

There are also points where the ideals and values of the two faiths converge in the commitment to live according to serious ethical norms which help to develop our own selves through respect for others. And I have suggested above that there may, too, be areas – such as environmental issues, religious pluralism and animal welfare – where Christians can learn from the insights and experience of this ancient yet strikingly contemporary faith.

Questions for Discussion

What can Christians learn from the Jain principle of *ahimsa* (non-violence) for the way they live their lives?

Can a Christian case be made for vegetarianism?

Where do Christian and Jain views of human origins and human destiny agree and where do they differ?

Chapter Five

Jews in Britain: a Way of Walking

Nick Sissons

The Jews in Britain: then and now

History & Law - a key date for modern British Jewry is 1656 when an edict of 1290 banning Jews from England was gradually set aside. The fledgling Jewish population, based mostly in London, grew in size and influence into the eighteenth century and many of the structures of modern Anglo-Jewry date back to this time, for example the Chief Rabbinate (1709) and the Board of Deputies of British Jews (1760). But Jews had to wait until the Religious Disabilities Act of 1846 to enjoy political rights, Lionel de Rothschild becoming the first Jewish MP to take his seat in Parliament in 1858 . At present Britain has twenty one Jewish MPs, Michael Howard being perhaps the best-known.

Today, under English law, Jews have no special status except in regard to certain religious practices. Three of the most obvious are:

- in schools Jewish parents can withdraw their children from Christian worship and R.E.;

- in court a Jew can take an oath on the Hebrew Bible, without the New Testament;

- regulations on animal-slaughter allow for the continued practice of *Shechita*, the method of ritual killing by which meat is rendered *kosher* for consumption by observant Jews.

Population & Geography

Britain's Jewish population, only about 25,000 in 1850, grew to nearly 350,000 by 1914, as Jews fled systematic massacres in the Russian Empire. After 1933 the number increased again because of Nazi persecution. Today it is in gradual decline, numbering in 2000 about 285,000. The fall has been caused by emigration, notably to Israel, and a growing trend of 'marrying out': when Jewish men marry non-Jewish (Gentile) women, their children are regarded as Gentiles under Jewish law, a Jew being traditionally defined only as someone who either has a Jewish mother or who has converted to Judaism. To halt this decline, some liberal Jews wish to define a Jew as anyone whose mother or father is Jewish.

Today's Anglo-Jewish population is still focused on London (196,000), which has the largest Jewish community of any European city apart from Paris (350,000). But significant communities also exist in other areas of the UK, notably around Manchester (26,000), in Leeds (8,000), Brighton & Hove (5,300) and Glasgow (5,600). However, the number of British Jews is tiny when compared to those living in the USA (5,800,000) and in Israel (6,145,000).

Issues that divide Jews

There are three main divisions within Jewry that correspond to three questions: Where do you live? Where did you come from? What do you believe?

Where do you live?

Throughout Jewish history enormous emphasis has been placed upon living 'in the land' promised to Abraham in the book of Genesis, chapter 15. But ever since the Babylonian conquest over 2,500 years ago, major Jewish centres have arisen outside 'the land' and there has been a conscious awareness of Jews living either 'in the land' or 'in the Diaspora'. The word 'diaspora' means 'a scattering' and the term Diaspora Jews, therefore, refers to those Jews who live outside Israel. This distinction remains alive today and because the State of Israel allows any Jew to return to the land by the Law of 'Aliyah' (literally 'going up') there are intense disagreements between those who feel every Jew should make 'Aliyah' and those who choose to remain in the Diaspora. Israeli Jews sometimes accuse those who stay in peaceful countries like the USA or the UK of 'suffering in style'. A significant moment was reached in the year 2000, when, for the first time since the biblical era, Israel became home to a greater number of Jews than any other country in the world, finally outnumbering the USA. This marks an enormous psychological turning point in world Jewry.

Where did you come from?

The main scatterings of Jews in post-biblical times were northwards and westwards. This gave rise to two main ethnic groupings: Ashkenazi Jews, who trace their roots back to Eastern Europe and Sephardi Jews, whose roots lie in Spain and North Africa. Ashkenazi and Sephardi customs and worship differ and long-standing tensions between the two groups sometimes surface in today's political and religious arenas. Anglo-Jewry is overwhelmingly Ashkenazi in origin; less than 3% of British Orthodox Jews come originally from Sephardic backgrounds. The differences in these two groupings can be detected in their style of synagogue. If you can visit London, compare the famous 'Bevis Marks' Sephardi synagogue built in 1701 with the Ashkenazi Central Synagogue originally erected in 1870 and rebuilt after the blitz in 1958.

What do you believe?

Religious Jews of nearly all descriptions are bound together by a common rhythm of life, organized around their weekly recognition of the sabbath, their lectionary cycle of prayers and scripture readings and their observance of annual feasts and commemorative days.[1] Yet there are certain theological differences which are so marked that they cause bitter divisions, even violence. But what is it that can cause co-religionists to set fire to each other's synagogues or attack Jewish women praying at the Western Wall, events which both occurred in the summer of 2000? This greatest and most sensitive of differences takes us to the heart of Jewish belief and arises, perhaps predictably, from conflicts over scriptural interpretations. To explain the situation we need to explore at some depth one of Judaism's key concepts, that of 'Torah'.

Torah

'Torah': 'God's guiding way'

Setting aside the Trinitarian formulas of the Gentile church, the Jewish concept of God remains in many ways identical to that espoused by Christianity, which is hardly surprising since Jesus and the first Christians were all Jews. Thus God is the good eternal Creator, transcendent yet immanent, graciously revealing himself through nature, history, Scripture and Spirit. But Judaism, unlike Christianity, understands obedience to God in terms of doing rather than believing the right things i.e. orthopraxy rather than orthodoxy.

The Jewish faith has, therefore, been called 'a way of walking' and *halakah* (the Hebrew word for 'walking') is the crucial ongoing task by which rabbis continue to relate the biblical commandments (*mitzvot*) to the changing circumstances of modern Jews. These *mitzvot* are contained in the 'Torah', a word often translated as 'Law', but which means 'Teaching' and refers to the ways by which God gives guidance to humanity. To study and act upon 'Torah' is the delightful yoke of being a Jew. When the poor man Tevye imagines the benefits of being rich he sings: 'And I'd discuss the holy books with the learned men seven hours every day; this would be the sweetest thing of all'.[2]

Torah is used in Judaism primarily to describe that divine teaching given to Moses on Sinai and enshrined in the first five books of the Bible; the word is also used of the scroll on which these books are written, which is every synagogue's holiest possession. But when the Romans drove the Jews out of Jerusalem, a generation after the death of Jesus, the meaning of Torah was gradually extended, first to include all other biblical material, for example the Prophets and Psalms, and then certain authoritative legal decisions and theological reflections of the rabbis of the time. These became called the 'Oral Torah' to distinguish them from the earlier 'Written Torah'. The 'Oral Torah' was itself written down later on in a huge collection of literature called the Talmud, whose modern edition of some 15,000 pages forms, with the Hebrew Bible, the backbone of Jewish religious thought and practice today.

Torah from heaven

The main conflict between contemporary religious Jews concerns whether or not they accept the traditional doctrine called in Hebrew *Torah min Hashamayim* (The Torah from heaven) which states that God gave to Moses on Sinai not only the 'Written Torah' but also the 'Oral Torah'. In other words, God revealed not only what is recorded in the books of Moses, but in essence everything that was later to be taught about those books by generations of rabbis, centuries after Moses was dead. This doctrine, which clearly presupposes a supernatural explanation of events, began to be questioned in the period known as the 'Haskalah' or the Jewish Enlightenment. In the late eighteenth century the USA's Bill of Rights (1787) and the French Revolution (1789) opened up the concept of who is a citizen and allowed groups hitherto excluded to play a fuller role in societies, whose new-found delight in Science and Reason was radically challenging cherished beliefs. As Jews began to leave the ghettoes, their spiritual world was confronted by this new 'enlightened' thinking. The fundamental challenge for them was: could they continue to believe all the Torah said when they lived in a world so different from those who wrote it? Could they carry on accepting traditional doctrines, formulated in a pre-scientific age, which did not square with their new perception of reality?

Although these challenges were basically the same for both Jews and Christians, the consequences of rejecting traditional beliefs were and remain very different: for Jews to reject the doctrine of 'the Torah from heaven' is effectively to reject the fundamental justification for the whole shape of Jewish religious life, which centres on the correct observance of the commandments of Torah. Many Jews would argue that to set aside such observance is to rip the heart out of Judaism, whilst their opponents would argue that honesty demands that they update belief in the light of modern knowledge.

The reforming movements

So Jewry is split theologically: those who accept 'the Torah from heaven', have become called 'observant' or 'Orthodox' Jews; those who do not are 'Non-Orthodox', represented by the Reform and the Liberal and Progressive traditions. Because these have rejected the doctrine, they have also waived observance of many of the 613 commandments found in the Torah. The reforming movement in Britain began in the 1840s with the establishment of the West London synagogue. At the inaugural service the rabbi (not surprisingly) preached on 'the Torah from heaven' and was promptly (and also not surprisingly) excommunicated by the Orthodox community!

There is one other main group within Judaism, called 'Masorti' or 'Conservative'. It regards itself as Orthodox, but, although Masorti Jews are observant, many Orthodox Jews reject them because they question scriptural tradition. Thus they occupy something of a middle position. In the UK, as in Israel, most religious Jews are 'Orthodox', unlike in the USA where Reform Jews dominate. There are, of course, many different sub-groups, the most visible being the 'Strictly Orthodox' whose style of dress is so distinctive. Because of their rigid stance towards modernity, this tiny fraction of British Jewry generally regard even the majority of 'Orthodox' Jews as hopelessly compromised by the way they have assimilated to the lifestyle of Western society.

Judaism does not think of itself in terms of denominations and, therefore, arguments between opposing groups are often couched in bitter terms of who is and is not a Jew. When the Reform rabbi Hugo Gryn died in 1997, the Orthodox Chief Rabbi, Jonathan Sacks, found himself trapped between on the one hand trying to honour this respected and much-loved national figure, and on the other placating those in his own community who regarded Rabbi Gryn as a heretic and not a real Jew at all. The fall-out from the Chief Rabbi's inability to hold both these in tension is still being felt amongst Anglo-Jewry and, despite continuing efforts to heal the wounds, may yet lead to the non-Orthodox Jews choosing their own Chief Rabbi in future.

Synagogue affiliation in the UK

At present in the UK, 40% of the 285,000 Jews belong to an Orthodox synagogue and 17% to a Non-Orthodox. This means that well over a third of all British Jews do not have any religious affiliation. In addition, many who hold synagogue membership do not regularly attend services except on the High Holy Days each autumn. This pinpoints an important fact: for many Jews, to be a Jew is about belonging not believing; religious observance is a means of identifying with their community rather than an expression of faith. Those outside looking in on the Jewish community need to grasp this, since Christianity in Britain, for example, is a faith you opt into whereas Judaism is not; if you are born Jewish and do not convert to another faith, then Jewish you remain, even if you never darken the synagogue door. However, because Jewish identity is so bound up with religious history, even secular Jews find themselves behaving religiously, for example many observe the Sabbath to some degree. As a result of the Nazis' attempt to exterminate European Jewry, many Jews also regard simply existing as a Jew or having Jewish children as a religious act of commitment. The Jewish theologian Emil Fackenheim went as far as to frame a 614th commandment to this effect: 'The authentic Jew of today is forbidden to hand Hitler yet another posthumous victory'.[3]

Issues that unite Jews

Although many things divide the Jewish community, two things draw them together: Israel and anti-Semitism. In the year 2000 the State of Israel celebrated its 52nd birthday and for most Jews the existence of Israel is of inestimable significance in the light of a long history of anti-Semitic persecution and violence, culminating in the Holocaust. Israel, therefore, represents a place where Jews are safe to be Jews. Thus, whilst many British Jews may dislike the particular government in power in Israel, this does not detract from their general support for the existence

People of Jewish and Christian faith together in the grounds of the Jerusalem citadel with Teddy Kollek.

Orthodox Jews celebrating a boy becoming 'bar-mitzvah', Western Wall, Jerusalem.

of the state itself. In April 2000 the high-profile but unsuccessful libel case brought by David Irving against those accusing him of denying the Holocaust was a reminder of the widespread activity of revisionist historians who, along with neo-Nazi groups, still seek to claim the Holocaust never happened. In some European countries, such as France and Germany, 'Holocaust Denial' is illegal, but Britain has so far refused to legislate against it, arguing that present legislation about incitement to racial hatred is sufficient. However, the institution of a Holocaust Memorial Day in Britain, to be held on the anniversary of the liberation of Auschwitz, January 27th, begun in 2001, demonstrates official commitment to the campaign to ensure events are not forgotten.

As time passes and the horrors of the Holocaust are put into greater perspective, so more Jews are critically addressing issues surrounding the Israeli treatment of Palestinians: whatever the evils perpetrated against the Jews in the past, this cannot exonerate evils committed by Jews in the present. For many Jews, especially the dwindling number of survivors, the scars of the Holocaust will never heal, but, in the younger generations, one detects a growing urgency to deal with Israeli injustices, lest the Jews seem to have forfeited any moral right to be 'in the land'. This explains mixed feelings expressed inside and outside the Jewish community over the introduction of a British Holocaust Memorial Day. Some people are concerned, of course, that it will attract the activities of neo-Nazis, but others are worried that it may lead to the neglect of other 'holocausts', committed elsewhere in the twentieth century, for example in Armenia, Vietnam and Rwanda. Inevitably, such re-evaluation of the Holocaust, along with criticism of Israel, leads to bitter arguments and accusations of anti-Semitism within Jewish communities.

Issues facing Christians in relations to Jews

Although the Jewish community of Britain is relatively small, the simple fact of its existence raises many issues for thinking Christians. I finish this article by briefly outlining eight things which I believe Christians need to do:

1   Recognize Judaism as a living dynamic faith and not as an obsolete ancient religion confined to the Bible; Jews are rightly offended when Christians are only interested in them as a way of learning more about the Church's roots. A visit to a synagogue or a regular read of the *Jewish Chronicle* weekly newspaper can be the beginning of a fresh appreciation of the vibrant Jewish community.

2   Realize that there are authentic Jewish interpretations of the 'Old Testament' (often pre-dating Christian interpretations) which have a validity of their own. This is not to say that Christian interpretations are wrong, but for Christians to claim that the Jews do not understand their own scriptures is as offensive as it is false.

3   Avoid uninformed caricatures about the differences between the two faiths such as: 'Judaism is about law and works and Christianity is about faith and grace'; 'the Old Testament reveals a God of Wrath, but the New Testament a God of Love' etc.. Ask a Jew what he/she really believes and begin to grapple with the complexity of the situation.

4   Appreciate Jesus' Jewishness and investigate the background of the conflicts that existed between Jews and early Christians, which influenced the writing of the gospels and Paul's letters.

5   Become familiar with the unjust treatment of Jews by the European churches over many

centuries, that was fuelled by a gross ignorance of Judaism and by the so-called 'teaching of contempt' derived from hostile passages in the New Testament, which claimed that God had rejected the Jews, that they were the devil's children and that by crucifying Christ they were responsible for the 'death of God'.

6   Read and reflect upon that strand of post-war Christian thinking, which seeks to affirm that God's covenant with the Jews is still valid (what has been called 'God's Yes to the Jewish No to Jesus') and struggles to understand how the survival of the Jews and their return to 'the land' might be part of God's will.

7   Become sensitive to the complex history and political instability of modern Israel and resist simply setting one side off against the other; the issue of the Jews living ethically in the land alongside the Palestinians is a real concern to many within Judaism.

8   Celebrate what Christians and Jews share as people of faith and strive to work together on issues of peace and justice in a largely secular society.

Some topics for discussion

1.   Spend some time in your group identifying who has or has had either personal contact with Jews or a working knowledge of their beliefs and practices. What impact has either the contact or knowledge had upon your self-understanding as a Christian or on your Christian thinking?

2.   Explore the ways in which Jews differ in their understanding of the nature of scripture. Do you think it is possible to hold together these varying views? Compare experiences from your own faith tradition. Do you think there should ever come a point when one Jew says to another 'You are no longer a Jew'? If so at what stage is that point reached?

3.   'Many Jews would argue that to set aside such observance (of all the commandments of Torah) is to rip the heart out of Judaism, whilst their opponents would argue that honesty demands that they update belief in the light of modern knowledge.' (quoted from Section 3 on 'Torah') Try and imagine yourself in the different positions highlighted here. Find out some concrete examples where Orthodox and Reform practices differs, for example over diet, Sabbath regulations, marriage, the role of women etc and ask yourself which arguments you find the more convincing and why.

4.   Many church statements since the last World War reflect changes in Christian attitudes to Judaism. See if you can discover how some of these changes have made their way into revised church liturgy, for example look at the Church of England's most recent liturgy for Good Friday and the new Methodist Church's Covenant Service. Try and find out what is the reasoning behind any changes you discover. Can you find other examples where recent changes of thinking in this area have been incorporated into liturgies and hymns? Can you find examples of hymns and prayers (old and new) which do not take note of these changes?

Notes

1.   See, for example, in *Teach Yourself Judaism*, the chapters on the Sabbath & the Festivals, C.M. Pilkington, Hodder & Staughton, 1995.
2.   'If I were a rich man' by Sheldon Harnick from the musical 'Fiddler on the Roof', 1964
3.   *The Jewish return into history*, Emil Fackenheim, Schocken Books 1978.

Chapter Six

The Muslims

David Craig

Introduction

When, in the wake of the publication of Salman Rushdie's book *Satanic Verses*, John Bowker, the Dean of Trinity College, Cambridge and I made the series of programmes *What Do Muslims Believe?* we began with comments from people about their understanding of Islam. The caricatures were all there: fundamentalists, shrouded women, public executions, intolerant ayatollahs, book burning and hostage taking terrorists. Well over a decade later the same caricatures are still being fuelled by stories such as the mass murder of holiday makers in the peaceful temples of the Nile and of bombings in Dar es Salaam, Nairobi and Capetown.

For a religion which claims one billion believers, such misunderstandings and inaccuracies are unforgivable. No wonder the Muslim communities of the West accuse their traditionally Christian neighbours of marginalisation, distortion, misrepresentation and even Islamophobia.

Christian relationships with Islam go back centuries. When Muhammad received the first revelations of what was to become the Qur'an in his cave on Mount Hira, the Christians were recognised as those 'nearest in love' to Muslims. With Jews and Zoroastrians, Christians were *peoples of the book*, because they too had accepted a divine revelation from God.

The Qur'an

Islam accepts the Qur'an as the absolute word of God with its teaching that, while other civilisations received revelations of this Word of God, only the Qur'an is the original, perfectly preserved. While the Jews had distorted their revelation by making of God an austere demanding judge, the Christians had betrayed their revelation of the truth by associating to God a son, and making the person of Jesus something divine - anathema to Islam which believes in the Unicity of a divine being, the Uniqueness and Oneness of God.

No Christian reading the Qur'an can fail to identify biblical parallels. While Judaism came from Abraham through his lawful wife Sarah, Islam came through Hagar and her son Ishmael. Many of the prophets are there, some more important than others. There is a graphic and sensual explanation of Potiphar's wife's accusation that Joseph had attempted to seduce her in the absence of her husband which casts light on the biblical account:-

> The Governor's wife *has been soliciting her page; he smote her heart with love, we see her in manifest error* but Joseph was going to be no one's toy boy - and as a result ends up in prison - *if his shirt has been torn from before, then she has spoken truly, but if the shirt is torn from behind then she has lied, and he is one of the truthful* - Needless to say his shirt was torn at the back as he ran from Mrs Potiphar! (sura 12:23-30)

More space is given to accounts of Mary in the Qur'an than in the Bible while the stories concerning Jesus seem to owe more to apocalyptic than canonical gospels - how as a child he created little birds of clay, breathed on them and sent them flying off into the air. [sura 5:110]

The crucifixion is recounted, but, because Jesus was a prophet, the beloved of God, he could not suffer so ignominious a death so, in a verse extremely difficult to interpret or translate, the Qur'an recounts how *they did not slay him, neither crucified him, only a likeness of that was shown to them.* (sura 4 155 -157) Islamic exegetes have suggested it was Judas Iscariot or even Pilate who took on the likeness of Jesus.

For Christians it would be easy to read the Qur'an as a distortion of the Bible. But such a reading would be to insult Islam. For Muslims, the Qur'an is their specific revelation of God in a way which Christians can only understand when they consider their relationship to Jesus Christ. Jesus is the Word of God as well as the Son of His Father. For Muslims, the Qur'an is the Word of God, co-existent with Him and preserved from eternity to be revealed to different civilisations at different points in the world's history.

There is much discussion about the means of the revelation. It has been suggested that Muhammad himself was illiterate but this seems doubtful as, before his marriage to the wealthy Khadija, a businesswoman, he had been her business manager, leading caravans along the trading routes to Syria and beyond and must have had some considerable numeracy and one assumes literacy. However, the very first word of the Qur'an is *Iqra' Recite!* and the Qur'an is an oral Arabic revelation which when written loses some of the impact. Muslims would argue that it cannot be translated, which is why A. J. Arberry's English edition of the Qur'an was called *The Qur'an Interpreted*.

The Qur'an itself can be divided into two parts. The early revelations are from the period in Mecca, apocalyptic and terse, concerned with God and his messenger and with graphic visions of hell-fire and gardens of paradise. The latter, longer revelations come from the time the community was establishing itself in Medina and contains codes of practice, ad hoc reactions to historical events and some detail of the times of, or the nature of, the revelations. Most of the background is left to the *Traditions,* the *Ahadith* - collections of stories about the time and life of Muhammad and his early followers, the only source of biography. There is no specific sanctity attached to Muhammad himself, although he is revered as the prophet to whom the Qur'an was revealed.

The Holy Prophet

Most religions grew over centuries and were influenced by many cultures and languages but Islam was revealed and its interpretation crystallized within a century. Muhammad lived from 570 to 632 CE but did not receive the first revelation until 610. Therefore, Islam's basic belief and codes of practice were constituted in just twenty years. They were also formed in a small triangle of land between Medina and Mecca, trading stations on the great routes of Arabia Felix. So perhaps it is not difficult to understand Islam's coherence, its dependence upon Arabic and the limited interpretations which have been given to it.

Muhammad was born in Mecca, the posthumous son of his father, and brought up by his influential grandfather Abd al Muttalib. Even as a young boy Muhammad was remarkable, receiving a vision where two angels, opening his chest, 'stirred their hands inside'. He was employed by the rich widow Khadija to take her trading caravans to Syria where a Christian monk Baqira identified in the youth signs of the promised Messiah.

At the age of twenty five he married his employer who bore him six children. The first two, sons, died in infancy and, of the four daughters, only one, Fatima, survived the Holy

Prophet. Scholars argue that the combination of his functional upbringing and the long lonely journeys through the desert heightened his spiritual awareness. Certainly he met with Jews and Christians as he travelled and became influenced by the *Hanifs*, a group of people who, in the polytheistic society of Mecca, sought to preserve a form of monotheism originating with Abraham.

At this time, Mecca was a major pilgrimage centre attracting many travellers to worship at the shrines of the thousands of idols contained in the *Ka'aba*, or Cube, that had been built to house a meteorite which had fallen on Mecca 'in the time of Abraham', giving the city its renown together with the basis for its successful commercial life. The tension between opulent paganism with its Corinthian pleasures and the austerity of monotheism caused Muhammad to retreat to a local cave on Mount Hira where the first revelation of the Qur'an was impressed upon him with both physical and mental intensity and he was urged to 'Recite':

Recite in the name of your Lord who creates man from a drop: Recite for your Lord is most generous, who teaches by the pen, teaches what he knows not (Sura 96: 1-5)

Fearing for his sanity, Muhammad took refuge with his wife who encouraged him to test the truth. Gradually further revelations came and Muhammad began to preach with an absolute sense that, 'if God is God, then there can only be what God is; there cannot be a God of the Christians, a God of the Jews, still less can there be the many deities of Mecca.' As a corollary, if God is one and the creator of all, then all people are part of one family, one community - the *umma* - whose every action should witness to the fact that there is no God but God, and Muhammad is his messenger.

The Growth of Islam

Only slowly did people begin to listen and accept this message. His wife, then Ali his cousin and Zayd his servant were first, then Abu Bakr. They were called *al-Muslamin*, Muslims, who enter a condition of safety because of their commitment to God. Persecution of the *al-Muslamin* grew and in 622 the little group escaped from Mecca to Yathrib (subsequently known as Medina - *Medinat an nabi,* the town of the prophet) where they were able to establish a community of believers.

Bearing in mind the size and universal presence of Islam today it is difficult to imagine its inauspicious beginnings. In the seventh century, Arabia contained small tribes each maintaining independence and surviving by raiding or trading and the only way the young Muslim community could survive was to raid caravans of the Meccan traders who had hounded them from the city. Those early days of Islam were marked by pitched battles culminating in the Muslim capture of Mecca and the cleansing of the *Ka'aba* of all its idols.

Muhammad died leaving no obvious heir in 632 and was succeeded by what Islam call the 'Four Rightly Guided Caliphs' who established Islam as the religion of the Middle East, finalised the canon of the Qur'an and began the collection of the *ahadith* which remain the earliest history of Islam and of its prophet.

With the establishment of Islam in Mecca and the effective submission of the opposition, it became possible to work out in practice the original revelation that 'there is no God but God and Muhammad is his messenger', the only credal formula in Islam. This *shahada* - witness - provides the first of the 'Five Pillars' which give Islam its form and all Muslims a structure for

The Badshahi Mosque, Lahore, Pakistan

their lives. The other four Pillars are the five daily hours for prayer, the alms tax or *zakat* payable by all adult Muslims, the fast during the month of Ramadan (the month during which the first revelation of the Qur'an was received) and the pilgrimage, the *hajj,* to Mecca and Medina to be undertaken at least once in a lifetime.

Islam in Britain

The Muslim community as it is found in Great Britain arrived in four waves. Early in the nineteenth century, seamen from South Asia and traders from the Middle East established communities around ports such as South Shields, Liverpool and Cardiff. After the First World War, Muslims who had served in the armed forces settled in Britain, bringing families and establishing communities. After the Second World War, Muslims came from India and Pakistan providing much needed labour in textile mills and factories and settling in the East End of London and the textile towns. With the implementation of Africanisation in newly independent African states during the 1970s, another wave of Muslims of Asian ethnic origins migrated to Britain, mainly from Kenya and Uganda.

The 1991 census identifies between 1 and 1.5 million Muslims in Britain and while the major centres of the community are in the Midlands, Yorkshire, Lancashire, London and Scotland, almost every town has its Muslim community. According to the publication *Religions in the UK - a Multi Faith Directory* there are some six hundred mosques registered in the United Kingdom.

The Muslim community is theologically divided between *sunni* and *shi'a* and perhaps these two schools might be compared with the Eastern and Western traditions of Christianity, as heirs to a common revelation but interpreting that revelation differently. The *sunni*, traditionalists, represent 90% of the world's Muslims, follow the *sunna* - the tradition, the way in which the prophet and his companions lived and behaved - and accept the first Four Rightly Guided Caliphs as the leaders of Islam.

The *shi'a* - (a word meaning party) represent only 10%. They believe that leadership of the Islamic community should have been hereditary and therefore that, after Ali's death, his sons Hassan and Hussein should have inherited the Caliphate. They accept the infallibility of the Caliph and believe that Ali's true successor went into hiding and as a 'hidden Imam' will return and overthrow an unjust civil order, against which the true believer has always been in opposition. Such belief explains and justifies such events as the support given to Ayatollah Khomeni and the success with which he was able to overthrow the corrupt regime of the Pahlavi dynasty. The *shi'a* are fragmented into many smaller groups marked by loyalty to a charismatic leader, for example the Aga Khan.

Islamic history has been marked by the missionary activity of both groups and *sunni* and *shi'a* dynasties have existed simultaneously from the beginning of Islam.

While second, third and fourth generations of British Muslims play prominent roles in British life, a strong identity with a country of origin is maintained: its fortunes and developments watched with interest and support. Legislation now allows for the establishment of Islamic education in Britain, and its support by the state, at long last giving the Muslim community equality with their Christian and Jewish partners. Yet, a report on Muslim presence in Britain published by the Runnymede Trust in 1997, *Islamophobia,* did suggest that the Muslim community in Britain is misunderstood and discriminated against. There is now an ongoing

Eid Congregation in the main courtyard of the London Central Mosque.

'Commission on British Muslims and Islamophobia'.

Points to Ponder

While some international manifestations of Islamic enthusiasm may be distortions of real Islam and need to be seen in context (no-one could ignore the Iranian revolution, the Palestinian *intifada*, the abuse of the Law in places such as Pakistan and Nigeria which has led to the persecution of Christians, and the extreme practice of the Taliban) any reading of the foundations of Islam, the Qur'an, the traditions of the prophet and the legal codes on which the practice of everyday life is based, reveal quite a different picture. Islam was a religion which restored to women their rightful place in society, and while recognising the finality of the revelation of the Qur'an, recognised, accepted and often encouraged discussion with other religions, allowing their existence and observance within the boundaries of Islamic states. It can be argued, for instance, that the Jews had greater security under the Ottoman Empire than under some Christian powers.

The gap between the ideal and the practical is always large. Which Christian community reflects the example of its founder? Current Islamic practices highlighted as extremist or fundamentalist must be seen in context and, when engaging in conversations with Muslims, Christians should be aware of the original inspiration rather than the many distortions of practice which we read about. In spite of the presence of Islam within Great Britain, there is need for some careful analysis of attitudes, confession of ignorance and serious commitment to understanding one of the fastest growing, missionary religions of the world.

Chapter Seven

New Agers: the search for heaven on earth

Martin Eggleton

What does 'New Age' conjure up?: travellers encamped where they shouldn't; alternative therapies; crystals and tarot cards; astrological charts and channelling? Go to any large bookstore and you will see whole sections of New Age books. Go to some large shops and you will find a range of try-it-yourself products: candles, music tapes, crystals, rocks, herbs, tarot cards and astrological charts. Something like 25% of all religious books now are to do with the New Age and it is an expanding market.

What is it?

There are two major obstacles to overcome when trying to describe what the New Age Movement is. The first is one's own pre-suppositions and prejudices (including Christian ones). There are those who think that what goes under New Age is the harbinger of the very anti-Christ warned of in the Bible. The second is the difficulty of slotting the assortment of interests, concerns and therapies into a single category. The New Age family is extensive, from Gaia and Creation Mythology to aspects of the occult, from various forms of alternative therapies to spirituality (Celtic, Women's, Men's). Some elements have a transcendental or religious flavour, others are simply techniques to enhance self-worth or improve somatic health.

Professor Eileen Barker, a leading sociologist of religion and international expert on New Religious Movements thinks that what joins one New Age group or practice with another is 'family resemblance'. This may mean that two members of the family may have almost no resemblance to each other, but they may both resemble a third member. Yet, one generalization that could be made is that the philosophy behind the New Age Movement has much more to do with self-journeying and self-discovery than with dogma and orthodoxy of belief. The authors who shine in the New Age firmament include Sir George Trevelyan, Marilyn Ferguson, David Spangler, Shirley McLaine, William Bloom, Matthew Fox, Satish Kumar, Rupert Sheldrake, Peter Russell, Eileen Caddy, Petruska Clarkson and Liz Greene - a collection of philosophers, scientists and others including a film star and a Roman Catholic theologian!

Given the above definitions, some readers might readily admit that they would, after all, include themselves as associate members of the New Age family. Even the most respectable of churchgoers have been known to find benefit from the likes of aromatherapy, meditation, yoga, and reflexology!

The Old Age and the New

Barbara Storm, a contemporary writer and journalist, describes the New Age Movement as 'the search for heaven on earth', a search for an experience of the divine in the here and now and an engagement of body, mind and spirit with forces external and internal, both metaphysical and immanent. And many in the New Age family believe that heaven has come much closer in our time, our age.

According to most astrologers, we are now moving from the age of Pisces to the age of Aquarius. Way back in the thirteenth century CE, Joaichim of Fiore, a mystic, believed that

"Something like 25% of all religious books now are to do with the "New Age".

history was divided into three ages - the first, the age of the Father; the second, the age of the Son; and the third, the age of the Spirit, when people would live in a blissful earthly paradise and possess full knowledge of God - dare I add 'as the waters cover sea'?

Followers of the New Age Movement believe that, as we move into a new millennium, we are moving from the age of Pisces to the age of Aquarius. The musical 'Hair' reminded some of us in the 1960s, forty years ago, that the dawn of Aquarius was upon us! In this New Age, it is believed we will learn to see the universe as one. We will live in one world, a global village, where we live or die together. The old dualistic view of the universe, with its constructs of good and bad, left and right, male and female, will be replaced by a monistic view. All is one and one is all.

Ancient Origins

Some of the origins of this are not new at all. They can be traced back to ancient Egypt or Greece and perhaps to the Christian heresy of Gnosticism, which placed emphasis on a kind of knowing which came through being initiated into esoteric knowledge. The revelation that was thought to come through this knowing, this hidden *gnosis* which others in the world were not privileged to, was thought to free one from the fragmentary and illusory material world. Salvation for Gnosticism entailed a glimpse into the inner workings of the cosmos, a wisdom which is other. It enabled the initiate to have a clue in deciphering the riddles of heaven and earth. It is just such a Gnosticism that is having a current resurgence.

The influence of the major world religions can also be easily traced. Take Buddhism and Hinduism for example. Zen Buddhism has shaped some New Age thinking and practice with its emphasis on an experience of enlightenment which breaks down commitment and attachment to the logical and rational ordering of experience. The Hindu doctrines of re-incarnation and karma which stress that how you behave in this world affects your life now and in the future, likewise have an influence. Yoga and meditation are being widely practised in the Western world too.

There is also the influence of Taoism, a Chinese form of religion that believes that in and behind the phenomenal world lies the Tao, the unchanging principle. Taoism stresses the harmonious interplay of two forces: *yin* (the principle of passive receptivity) and *yang* (the principle of activity). More recently these have been interpreted as the female and male principles at work in the world. Then there are ancient traditions interspersed in the New Age practices stemming from Pagan, Native American, Druidic and Celtic traditions.

So the great religions, including Christianity - particularly its eschatological and apocalyptic elements that talk of moving to an end point with a new Heaven and a New Earth, with a language of 'the lamb lying down with the lion' and its secret mystery codes locked up in the Book of Revelation - have been truly stirred into the New Age pot.

More Recent Influences

In more modern times the New Age Movement has a number of precursors. The Transcendental Movement (1836-40) was one, shaped by people like Thoreau and Emerson in America who were deeply influenced by the wisdom of the East. The Transcendentalists borrowed from the Eastern scriptures, making them fit American standards of autonomy and individual determination. Both Transcendentalism and Unitarianism stressed human potentialities, the transcending impulse for self-realization, which is now prevalent in the New Age Movement, particularly through the

Human Potential Movement.

Then there was the rise of Spiritualism and the writings of people like Fanz Anton Mesmer (1734- 1815: hence mesmerism) that stimulated a new mental Healing Movement. Mesmeric sleep was taught and the role of hypnosis was developed. Psychic healers like Parkhurst Quimby and Mary Baker Eddy spread the teaching that disease was caused by false beliefs and not physical disorders. The Christian Science Church is its inheritor. This opened the door to the practices of clairvoyance, prophecy, and, especially in the USA, channelling.

Spiritualism was further developed as a movement through the Fox sisters in America and the influence of Madame Blavatsky and the advent of Theosophy, in the nineteenth century. According to the Theosophists, we are now in the fifth race of the seven root races, when human consciousness will unite with its spiritual soul. Theosophy went on to influence people like the poets Yeats and Eliot and the writer Bernard Shaw. There is a connection between Theosophy and Freemasonry and the Knights Templar.

Then there was the influence of Georgy Ivanovich Gurdjieff (1877-1949), the strange Russian mystic traveller, a philosopher, hypnotist and dancer. Still today people meet in London to propagate his teaching and practices, including his wild dancing. To Gurdjieff 'man is asleep'. Occasionally, in moments of peak intensity, he becomes self aware and catches a glimpse of his true potential.

Important Aspects

Of the many aspects of the New Age ethos, three can be highlighted.

New Science

The former mechanistic Newtonian view of the cosmos has given way to a more expanded and fluid view of reality. Matter and energy are seen bound together. There is one continuum. What is called the New Science in the New Age Movement links with this and is pre-eminently holistic. No longer are we to be seen as impartial observers of the natural world. Spectators and analysts are part of the observed. There is an interaction between observed and observer. A butterfly flapping its wings in one country affects the environment many miles away. So it is in the realm of human personality. The tradition is to divide human beings into the trichotomy of body, mind and spirit. In the New Age we are to view the person as a whole within a whole 'Gestalt'. So we must approach healing and medicine holistically, not simply in terms of palliative and symptom-based treatments but relating to the whole person in their whole environment. The so-called alternative or complementary therapies take centre stage in the New Age Movement.

Again, the old dichotomy between science and religion, between the left side and the right side of the brain, between the logical deductive and the intuitive and creative, between body and mind, between the somatic and the spiritual, is to be broken down. The New Science wants to do away with old ways of approaching science and to discover knowledge through the holistic approach.

Ecology

The New Age empathizes with the plight of the planet. It speaks of 'deep ecology' which explores the relationship between all forms of life in their profound spiritual and philosophical dimensions. The accent is on interdependence. The global environment is sensitive and balanced. This affects not only what we buy at the supermarket but our attitudes and moods.

Deep ecology urges us to recognize the world as 'Gaia', a kind of Mother Earth spinning in space, who lives and breathes as a complete organism, ecologically finely balanced, with us humans as part of that balance. The New Age Communities established in places like Findhorn in Scotland and the Esalen Institute in California seek to demonstrate the cosmic energy available to us to live more harmoniously with the natural world.

The New Psychology

New Age psychology takes not only the Freudian model of the subconscious but also the interaction of bodies and their language, the dynamics of the supraconscious, the transpersonal, the beyond, the paranormal and the psychical, and the findings of hypnotism and Neuro-Linguistic Programming. From the USA come the psychotherapeutic influences of people like Rogers and Maslow giving rise to the Human Potential Movement. In Britain, Gestalt, Psychosynthesis, Rational Emotive and Transactional Analysis are all popular counselling therapies as part of Humanistic Psychology.

The Popularity of the New Age Movement

For many in the West, religion has become too formalized, dogmatic, negative and rule-bound. It is seen as paternalistic and authoritarian. The appeal of New Age must be seen in this context. It affirms that human nature is more deprived than depraved. It embodies a real search for world affirmation, for ultimate, total awareness and bliss. There is a longing within it for being together in open, meaningful community. Communities like Findhorn, in Scotland, started by Eileen Caddy, in the 1960s, offer love, warmth, healing, community and hope to stress-worn, techno-abused people, without the constrictions of the theonomy of the church or synagogue.

James Lovelock's emphasis on Gaia is also very attractive to those who are in to Green issues: that Planet Earth is a sacred living planet which we are destroying and hurting and exploiting. The Earth has her own sensitivity and consciousness, New Age stresses. We are urged, then, to get in touch with our primal bonds - with the earth and the sea and the mountains, with water and fire and earth, practising chanting at sunrise, physical movements to the moon, touching trees, submerging ourselves in tubs of warm water in silence, chanting mantras etc.

We have at our disposal controls over nature and we can become masters of genetic engineering. We can reach to the deepest ocean and move out into space. The New Age Movement, however, stresses that human beings are stewards of the world not exploiters who can dominate and subdue it.

Christian Criteria

Christians would agree that what is needed is a change of heart: a change of heart and mind and body and soul that turns around our attitudes, that values life, that believes that we are sisters and brothers inhabiting this spinning globe together, that we have to be reconciled to Creation.

The doctrine of Creation is one major talking point between Christians and New Age Spirituality. The Methodist Report to Conference on the New Age (1994) points out that ***'any Christian doctrine of creation will need to be emphatically theocentric ... effected through and finding its integrating point in Christ'***. For New Agers, however, cosmic life appears as a self-enclosed system within which impersonal forces, rather than the dictates of a personal, purposive Creator, affect the direction of events.

And what about human nature? Christian Theology sees it as 'fallen', tainted with 'original sin' stemming from Adam's Fall. The New Age is basically optimistic. Man is asleep or unaware or at most deprived but he is not fallen, alienated, depraved. He is not tainted with sin. In the New Age, human nature is neither good nor bad but open to continuous transformation. There is only *can* not *can't*.

Christian Theology stresses the sovereignty of God and his power and control over all created things. Christians seek to know the will of this Divine Being and want to do the divine will rather than follow the dictates of human desire. In the New Age all things are possible. You can find the resources in yourself, the very same sources that keep the universe in flux.

For Christians, salvation or wholeness comes through divine intervention but it is appropriated in the here and now. Perhaps Christians, therefore, have a lot in common with New Agers. The Christian doctrine of fallenness and sin might be an area where we can begin to have dialogue with New Agers. We believe all things are possible. Whether or not we expect the New Age to dawn soon with the return of Jesus, is a matter of belief and scriptural interpretation. As Christians we look for a new heaven and a new earth. Saying the Lord's Prayer, we ask that God's kingdom arrive on earth 'as it is in heaven'.

We always live in the New Age if we believe that Christ is always making things new, even now.

Chapter Eight

The Sikhs

Joy Barrow

Introduction

There are twenty million Sikhs in the world today, of whom about sixteen to seventeen million live in India, mainly in the Punjab. The rest live outside India in, for example, Malaysia, Thailand, Canada, USA, Fiji, Kenya and Australia - as well as France, Germany and Britain.

Today there are approximately 400,000 to 500,000 Sikhs in the United Kingdom, the West London area having the largest community. People tend to have a stereotyped image of a Sikh as a turbaned man or a woman wearing the Punjabi shalwar kameez. However, this is somewhat simplistic. Many Sikhs who arrived in Britain immediately after the Second World War cut their hair in order to gain employment. Whilst some have subsequently grown it again, others still have short hair. Some Sikhs, especially among those born in Britain, have never worn their hair long. Furthermore some women wear turbans.

The Sikh Code of Conduct, the *Rahit Maryada*, defines a Sikh as 'Any person whose faith is in one God, the Ten Gurus and their teaching, and the Adi Granth. In addition, he or she must believe in the importance of *amrit* (initiation) and must not adhere to any other religion. Sikhism is concerned with individual life and corporate life as a member of the Sikh community.'

Sikhism is a monotheistic religion which traces its origins to the divinely inspired words, or *gurbani*, of Guru Nanak (1469-1539). The word 'Guru' is often translated as 'teacher', but this is inadequate. The explanation Sikhs give is that it comes from two Punjabi words, 'gu' meaning darkness and 'ru' meaning 'light'. A Guru is therefore someone who delivers a person from the darkness of misunderstanding and ignorance to spiritual enlightenment. Consequently, the word Guru may refer to God (who has a variety of names including *Vahiguru* and *Satguru*), the Ten Human Gurus, and the holy scriptures, the Guru Granth Sahib.

Guru Nanak and Nine Others

Sikhs believe that Guru Nanak was called into God's presence at the age of thirty and told to 'go into the world to pray and teach humanity how to pray'. For the next thirty years, he travelled extensively, teaching people by both his actions and words to meditate on God's name, or the whole personality of God (*nam simran*); to earn a living through honest work and to give a proportion of what they earnt to those in need (*dan*); to practice cleanliness, or to keep clean and tidy for reasons of hygiene and not ritual washing (*isnan*); and to practice service to both God and humanity as a whole, not just other Sikhs (*seva*).

Guru Nanak always took a Muslim friend, Mardana, with him on his travels. Mardana was a musician who played a rebeck, a stringed instrument rather like a mandolin. Whenever Guru Nanak spoke the *gurbani*, or God's words, Mardana composed a tune to fit them. The compositions of Mardana are the origin of the Sikh tradition of *kirtan*, or the singing of religious songs.

Wherever Guru Nanak went, places of worship called *dharamsalas* were established where

Nam simran: A Sikh meditating on the kirtan which he hears coming from the Golden Temple.

Photo: Joy Barrow

the *sangat*, or community of believers, met together for *nam simran* and to share a meal. Guru Nanak believed that it was only by practising *nam simran* that liberation from the cycle of birth-death-rebirth could be achieved. There are different levels of *nam simran*. At the first stage, the person repeats a word, for example *Vahiguru*, or a daily prayer, but does so with little thought of what is being said.[1] At the second stage, the person takes part in *diwan*, or the worship ceremony in the gurdwara, singing *kirtan*. At the third stage, God's word is interiorised. This is a spiritual development, beyond explanation and description, which can only be experienced, and is achieved through a deep contemplation of God's mystery.[2]

In about 1520 Guru Nanak settled in Kartarpur in the Punjab. There he established a community which had two characteristics: first, everyone lived a family life and, secondly, the focus of it was the words, or *gurbani*, of Guru Nanak. Before breakfast, in the afternoon and in the evening the *gurbani* was sung.

Guru Nanak was succeeded in turn by nine men. Succession was based on a person's spiritual qualities, not on hereditary grounds. The fifth Guru, Guru Arjan, supervised the collection of the *gurbani* of Guru Nanak and his successors, and those of some Hindu and Muslim holy men whose teachings were similar to those of Guru Nanak. In August 1604 this collection, known as the Adi Granth, was installed in the newly completed Harmandir Sahib (now sometimes referred to as the Golden Temple) in Amritsar. At the installation Guru Arjan made prostration to the Adi Granth, thereby showing that the *gurbani* was more important that he was, for it was God's Word while he was only a messenger of God.

The tenth Guru, Guru Gobind, added the *gurbani* of his father, the ninth Guru, Guru Tegh Bahadur, to the Adi Granth. Shortly before he died, Guru Gobind stated that there would be no more human Gurus but that the Adi Granth would be his successor. Consequently it became known as the <u>Guru</u> Granth Sahib.

The Gateway to the Guru

The Sikh place of worship is the called the gurdwara. This is a combination of two Punjabi words: *Guru* and *duara*. The word '*duara*' means gateway, consequently 'gurdwara' means 'the gateway to the Guru'. A gurdwara is therefore any place where the Guru Granth Sahib is installed. When visiting a gurdwara, clothes should modestly cover the legs and arms. Before entering, a person must take off his or her shoes and cover the head. Usually there is a supply of long scarves inside the main entrance. Although it covers the head, the wearing of baseball style caps is best avoided. Alcohol or tobacco should never be taken into the gurdwara.

Inside the gurdwara, the Guru Granth Sahib is in a central position at the front, placed on a small table on a raised platform or throne (*takht*). It will be covered in richly embroidered cloths, and a canopy will be above it. By the side of the *takht* there is a small platform for musicians, who will accompany the *kirtan*.

Upon entering, a worshipper will walk up to the Guru Granth Sahib, make prostration to it and give a gift, usually of money. It must be stressed that this is not an act of worship but is a sign of respect for the Guru Granth Sahib, as it is believed to be God's Word and the living presence of God among God's people. Visitors to the gurdwara may also wish to make prostration as a matter of courtesy, however this is not essential. Worshippers sit cross legged on the floor, usually men on one side and women on the other. Care should be taken not sit with your feet pointing towards the Guru Granth Sahib, or with your back to it, as these are both

Photo: Joy Barrow

The sukh asan ceremony, Amritsar: Carrying the Guru Granth Sahib in procession from the Golden Temple to the Akal Takht, where it rests for the night.

regarded as very disrespectful.

Visitors to a gurdwara are always made very welcome. If you are organising a group, it is advisable as well as courteous to telephone the gurdwara office before the visit. However, if you are attending as an individual this is not necessary. *Diwan*, the worship service, may last from two to several hours, but people come and go throughout; there is no concept of arriving at the beginning and staying until the end! *Diwan* consists of *kirtan* and several talks, called *katha*, based on the Guru Granth Sahib. The word *'kirtan'* comes from the word *'kirtat'*, which means 'praise'. In the Guru Granth Sahib it states, 'The eternal Lord, Eternal Name; The way to communicate is intense love.. Sing, listen to God's praises with inner love.[3]

There are three levels of *kirtan*. At its initial level, it is described as *kan-rasa,* which literally means 'pleasure of the ears'. This is when the *kirtan* cleanses the mind of its spiritual darkness and lower passions: 'Whoever chants or listens to kirtan, their dark thoughts vanish. All wishes are fulfilled and hope is strengthened'.[4] The second stage is when the mind becomes increasingly more attuned to the *kirtan*. When a person frequently experiences *kirtan* in this way, it brings about a state of *sahaj*, or spiritual equipoise. 'When the consciousness awakens to the melody of the *shabad* [or *gurbani*] within, the mind in the body is detached from worldly pleasures. The mind is attuned to the True Name. Devotion to God brings equipoise through the Guru's *shabad*; the Name tastes sweet and one is absorbed in it'.[5] The third, and highest, level of *kirtan* is *surat-shabad-da-mel*, which means the union of consciousness with God. 'Then the blissful strain creates the unstruck music. And through the spiritual experience of *shabad*, one realises the Pure Land'.[6]

At the end of *diwan* a pattern of events takes place. First, the congregation will stand and place their hands together at chest height while a congregational prayer called *Ardas*, which means petition, is said. Visitors should also stand out of courtesy. In about the middle, and at the end, of *Ardas* the congregation make prostration. *Ardas* will be followed by a *hukamnama*. This is a reading taken at random from the Guru Granth Sahib, which is believed to be God's message to the congregation. The first *hukamnama* which is taken each day, usually at dawn, is prominently displayed near the entrance to the *diwan* hall. It is a common sight throughout the day to see Sikhs standing in front of the words, meditating on them.

The service concludes with the eating of *karah parshad.* The ingredients are equal parts of semolina, butter and milk. Sikhs, however, often say that the extra ingredient is the *gurbani*, as it has been prepared in the presence of God's Word. *Karah parshad* will be given to all members of the congregation in their cupped hands, right hand above the left one. *Karah parshad* is a symbol of the Sikh belief in the equality of humanity; not to eat it is perceived as very disrespectful, although you can ask for a small quantity.

After *diwan*, worshippers eat a communal meal called *langar*, although it is available throughout the day to all visitors, both Sikh and non-Sikh. *Langar* is also a symbol of the equality of humanity. Sikhs frequently emphasise the importance of the *langar* by telling the story of the Mughal Emperor Akbar. One day he visited the third Guru, Guru Amardas. As the Emperor, Akbar expected immediately to be shown into the Guru's presence. However, he was commanded to sit on the ground with the other visitors and share a meal, for the rule of Guru Amardas was 'first eat together, then meet together'. *Langar* can also provide for the material needs of Sikhs and non-Sikhs. I am aware of several non-Sikhs who regularly have *langar* as their main meal of the day, as they know they can come to the gurdwara and eat, free of charge.

Some of the Sikh young people who meet weekly to read and study the Guru Granth Sahib at a West London gurdwara.
Note: The Guru Granths which are being studied are in two volumes, therefore they are placed on a reading stool; those in a single volume must always be installed on a takht, whether they are being read or resting for the night.

The Equality of Humanity

Equality of humanity is an important belief in Sikhism. Theoretically it allows no distinction between people on grounds of birth, race or gender. Any Sikh may perform any of the tasks in the gurdwara, from being President to serving at the *langar* and looking after the shoes. A visitor may see a man or a woman reading the Guru Granth Sahib, as anyone may do so if they are able to read the gurmukhi script it is written in. For this reason, the disagreements in the Church regarding the status of women are puzzling to Sikhs. Non-Sikhs may also be invited to speak to the *sangat*, as this writer has done, and some Sikhs do not understand why they are not given reciprocal treatment in churches. One Sikh, who is actively involved in inter-faith dialogue, has often said, "There can be no true inter-faith dialogue when I am not allowed in your pulpits". Some gurdwaras have a *granthi*, whose responsibility it is to read the Guru Granth Sahib and organise services in the gurdwara. However, this is for purely practical reasons. Although sometimes a *granthi* may be referred to as a priest, it is not in the sense of an ordained minister as the word would be understood in Christianity. In an effort to be helpful, confusion may in fact be created.

Service

Another important aspect of Sikhism, is *seva*, or service to God and humanity. The gurdwara is often called the laboratory of *seva*, as it provides many opportunities for service, for example, through preparing and serving the food in the langar, washing up the dirty dishes, looking after the shoes, or reading the Guru Granth Sahib. All are equally acts of *seva* and none is more important than another. *Seva* may, however, be participating in sponsored events or collecting money for charity. Two things must be stressed. First, it is the duty of all Sikhs to do *seva* and, secondly, *seva* is for the benefit of all humanity, not just other Sikhs.

The Khalsa: a way of living

Guru Gobind Singh is also important because, at the festival of Vaisakhi in 1699, he commanded all Sikhs to assemble before him at Anandpur. He then asked for a volunteer who would be willing to offer his head to the Guru. This was not only a challenge to those present to offer their lives to God but, as it was a time when Sikhs were being persecuted by and were at war with the Mughal Empire, it also represented an offer to serve in the army of Guru Gobind Singh. One by one, five Sikhs offered their lives. In turn, the first four volunteers were taken into a large tent and, after each of them, Guru Gobind Singh emerged alone with blood dripping from his sword. After the fifth volunteer was taken into the tent, all five came out dressed in saffron robes and wearing turbans. These five are known as the *panj piare,* or five beloved ones. Because of their willingness to sacrifice their lives, they are seen as exemplars of how Sikhs should live and were the first five members of the Khalsa. Guru Gobind stated that the Khalsa was to be a community of people who would combine the spirituality of a holy person, or *sant*, with the courage and bravery of a soldier, or *sipahi.*

Guru Gobind stated that Sikhs should live according to a Code of Conduct, or *Rahit*, which provided Sikhs with a religious and moral code. Among other things, the *Rahit* prohibits Sikhs from using tobacco and alcohol and, positively, instructs them to wear religious symbols known as the 5Ks. This is because K is the first letter of each item in Punjabi: *kesh* (uncut hair), *kara* (steel wrist band), *kangha* (comb), *kirpan* (sword) and *kachhahira* (loose shorts). Each of these items has deep spiritual meaning today. When the Offensive Weapons Act was passed, the wearing of the *kirpan* by Sikhs was specifically excluded from the Act's prohibitions. Although the wearing of the *kirpan* by school children may sometimes raise initial questions, it has proved perfectly possible to overcome concerns on the part of school and education authorities. Although the turban is not regarded as one of the 5Ks, it has a deep meaning for Sikhs and lengths of cloth for turbans are frequently exchanged as an act of respect, for example at marriage or when the head of a family has died. In 1976 Sikhs obtained the right to wear the turban in place of a crash helmet when riding a motor bike. In 1984, in a ground breaking ruling in the case of Mandla v Dowell, the House of Lords ruled that Sikhs were an ethnic group.[7]

Celebration

The festival of Vaisakhi is a time of celebration and Sikhs will visit the gurdwara, often from very early in the morning. The *nishan sahib* outside gurdwaras is changed every Vaisakhi. This is a saffron-coloured flag, which carries the Khalsa symbol in blue. In some towns, the Guru Granth Sahib is carried in procession through the streets. In Southall there are usually approximately 20,000 people in the procession that follows the scriptures. As 1999 was the tercentenary of the founding of the Khalsa, gurdwaras around the world organised additional celebrations to mark the event. As a permanent remembrance of the tercentenary, a group of Sikh young people from the Southall and Slough area in Britain founded Khalsa Aid. This is a humanitarian relief organisation which provides care for people regardless of their religion or country of birth. Its members have already taken relief supplies to Kosovo, and Turkey after the earthquake. When doing so, they have used their holiday allowance from their paid employment.[8]

The second major festival in Sikhism is that of Divali. Although it is a festival celebrated throughout India, for Sikhs it is a reminder of the return to Amritsar of the sixth Guru, Guru Hargobind, who had been unjustly imprisoned in the Gwalior Fort during the reign of Emperor Jehangir. When offered his freedom, he refused to leave until fifty two Hindu princes who had also been unjustly imprisoned were freed. The Mughal authorities agreed that as many princes as could hold onto the Guru's cloak would be released. With great wisdom, Guru Hargobind ordered a cloak with fifty two tassels to be made. Holding onto a tassel each, all the princes walked to freedom. By his actions, Guru Hargobind was exemplifying the Sikh respect for all faiths and its concern for all humanity.

Sikh-Christian Relationships

Today there are various activities which bring Sikhs and Christians together. Sikh-Christian scripture studies have regularly taken place for several years in West London. Furthermore, as a mark of respect for Cardinal Basil Hume, who was actively involved in inter-faith dialogue, the Ramgarhia gurdwara in Southall sponsored a memorial service for him on the day of his funeral in 1999 and, in 2000, the Nishkam Seva Jatha gurdwara in Birmingham organised an inter-faith conference. The year 2000 also saw the opening of the Birmingham University Centre for Christianity and Asian Religions at Selly Oak, within which input from the Sikh tradition has been high.

In these ways, and many others, dialogue between Christians and Sikhs is taking place for, while reading books can give a knowledge of a religion, it is only through people meeting people, that faith meets faith. So it is only as people visit gurdwaras, and meet Sikhs, that they will meet living Sikhism.

Notes

1   However, in some gurdwaras there is a one hour continuous recitation of Vahiguru from

about 4.00 a.m., where the word is used as a mantra and as a focus for meditating on God. It has been apparent on occasions when I have been present that a deeply spiritual practice was taking place.

2   W.H. McLeod: Textual Studies for the Source of Sikhism (Chicago, University of Chicago Press, 1990) p. 40.

3   AG p. 1. Unlike the Bible which is divided into chapters and verses, references to passages in the Guru Granth Sahib relate to the page number on which the passage is found, therefore AG p.1 indicates that the quotation is found on page 1. AG stands for Adi Granth, the name given to the Sikh scriptures which were first compiled under the supervision of Guru Arjan.

4   AG p. 683. See Gobind Singh Mansukhani, "The Unstruck Melody: Musical Mysticism in the Scripture" in Kerry Brown (ed.) Sikh Art and Literature (Routledge, 1999), pp. 117-128 at pp. 123-125.

5   AG p. 907.

6   AG p. 1042.

7   This case was regarding the refusal of a private school to admit a Sikh boy unless he wore the school cap, which would have meant him cutting his hair.

8   For further information, Khalsa Aid can be contacted at PO Box 1545, Slough, SL1, Berkshire, or e-mail: KhalsaAid@hotmail.com

Chapter Nine

The Zoroastrians: the call to recognize One Creator

Shahin Bekhradnia

The Beginnings

The founder of Zoroastrianism, Zarathushtra, or Zoroaster as the Greeks rendered the name, cannot be ascribed any precise date and dating is a hotly contested issue. Academic opinion, which bases its case on linguistic analysis of the oldest texts, suggests a date roughly around 1500 BCE. Other suggestions, based on Greek sources, arrive at dates as far apart as 6000 BCE and the sixth century BCE. Furthermore his exact place of origin cannot be pinpointed, although it is thought that he either lived in the part of Iran which is known as Azarbaijan today or possibly in what has been called Greater Iran, namely around Balkh, or possibly as far East as the Pamir mountains in today's Tajikistan. All these areas are connected by a common Iranian culture and once upon a time practised Zoroastrianism. Yet, today the Zoroastrian world population is no more than 150,000 with maybe 40,000 in Iran, and about 75,000 in India. The rest are dispersed in diaspora around the world, with the bulk in USA and Canada. In Britain, there are approximately 5-6,000 Zoroastrians resident in the country.

The corpus of Zoroastrian prayer texts, known collectively as the *Avesta,* provides both the ideas resulting from the divine revelation which came to Zoroaster and also historical background through which scholars try to contextualise his life. It contains layers of prayers in different languages, indicating additions at different times, and suggesting a tradition which underwent linguistic and occasionally philosophical transformation. The oldest of these languages is found in the *Gathas* which lies at the heart of the prayers and is thought to contain Zoroaster's own words. It is therefore this particular text above all other Zoroastrian literature which should be studied to appreciate the radical philosophy that Zoroaster propounded.

Persecution and Oral Transmission

When we speak of Zoroastrian texts, it should be borne in mind that there was apparently, according to later writings, a rich body of written religious texts and associated literary material kept in the palaces and temples of Iran, all of which were torched during the invasion of Alexander of Macedon in the third century BCE. In the centuries following this, the texts which had survived in more remote depositories were brought together and recompiled, undoubtedly aided by what had been memorized by priests. This led to the increasing importance that was given to priesthood training during which priests learned prayers and commentary by heart.

The texts, however, were burnt a second time alongside much else, this time by the Arabs during their invasion in the first half of the seventh century CE, which brought about the end of Iranian culture for about two hundred years and established the decline of Zoroastrianism amongst Iranian peoples. During the ensuing years many monarchs ordered surviving Zoroastrian books to be brought in, whereupon they were burnt or trampled underfoot in the presence of Zoroastrian priests. Thus oral recitation and faithful transmission by word of mouth assumed an even greater relevance.

Owing to this, the oldest manuscript of Zoroastrian literature is relatively recent, dating from the thirteenth century CE in spite of the religion's ancient origin. It should be noted that it was two European scholars, one a British polyglot William Jones, and the other a Frenchman, Anquetil du Perron, who managed to trace a relationship between the language of the older prayers and Sanskrit and therefore to establish them as Indo-European.

Zoroaster's Message

What made Zoroaster's ideas radical was firstly his revelation that there was one Creator, *Ahura Mazda*, the Wise Lord, at a time when it was commonplace to worship the numerous natural elements as gods in their own right. His understanding of life was based on his realization that all the manifestations of creation had to come ultimately from one all-powerful energy - God or the Self-Creator. His originality is further seen in his injunction found in the *Gathas*, that those who are listening should use their free will to choose their own path, that of good or that of evil. In this injunction are two fundamental ideas: free will and individual responsibility for one's own actions; the concepts of good and evil. Good and evil are understood as realities encountered in the inner mind - the conscience - that appear to operate as twin energies, equally present and both exerting a pull over us. Zoroaster's message was basically that we should be aware of the struggle these two forces engage us in, and know the consequences of following one rather than the other. We are told that to follow the path of righteousness *(asha)* or purity in thought, word and deed will lead to happiness *(ushta)* for both ourselves and others. The alternative choice of deceit, lies, and unkindness, namely impurity of thought, word and deed will lead to unhappiness, enmity and war. Thus Zoroastrians are engaged in an ethical dualism.

Zoroaster specifically exhorted men and women to use their own unclouded judgement to decide if what he, Zoroaster, advocated had a relevant message for them. It is particularly noteworthy that throughout the *Gathas* he addresses both men and women, indicating that they are partners in trying both to increase the amount of goodness and to defeat the forces of darkness. This equality of address implies respect towards both sexes and a belief in the competence of both. Indeed, lack of gender prejudice is one of the fundamental features of Zoroastrianism and is seen in societal organization, later non-prayer texts and even the wedding liturgy.

Eschatology

Zoroastrianism has had an impact that is rarely realized in the Christian world through its contribution to the concepts of heaven and hell, deriving from ethical dualism. This later developed into a more elaborate form in which ideas were misunderstood and *Ohrmazd (Ahura Mazda)*, God, was conflated with Good Thinking, *Spenta Mainyo*, and wrongly counterpoised with Bad Thinking, *Ahriman (Angra Mainyo)*. In other words, God was counterpoised with the Devil. Associated with this was the concept of the day of judgement at which point, on the third day/fourth night after death, the soul crossed a bridge, *Pol e Chinvat*, on which its good deeds were weighed against its bad deeds. The outcome of this balance determined whether one would pass through to the abode of eternal light and happiness, or be plunged off the bridge into an eternal abyss.

The Symbol of Fire

The energy of the Creator is represented in Zoroastrianism by fire or the sun, both of which embody many of the characteristics of the creative force. As the Creator, they are enduring, radiant, pure, and life-sustaining. For this reason, Zoroastrians pray in front of some form of

Photo: Shahin Bekhradnia

The Sacred Fire

light, preferably fire or the sun (or at night, the moon which reflects the sun), a candle or sometimes an electric light. All symbolize the Creator and focus attention totally so that thanksgiving, praise and contemplation of the wonders of creation can take place in serenity. In our places of worship, therefore, an urn containing fire which is kept alive by donations of fragrant sandalwood or myrrh is the most important feature. This practice of respecting fire has given rise to disrespectful accusations of idolatry and fire-worship, levelled at Zoroastrians by those whose interests were served in misrepresenting our approach to fire. Zoroastrians, however, see this practice as lying in the same category as the Christians' attitude towards the cross, which is worn around the neck and hangs or stands centre stage in most churches.

Nature and the Environment

In the *Gathas* there are several references to Mother Earth and the wonders of natural phenomena such as the moon, the stars, the wind and so on. Nature in fact is central to the practice of Zoroastrianism and understanding the interdependence of human life, the seasons and the elements lies at its core. Many of our important annual festivals are in celebration of nature: our new year on the first day of Spring (21 March); our water festival in Summer; our Autumn festival at the end of the season; our mid-Winter fire festival. It should be said that there are many days for feasting and celebrations to break up an otherwise laborious lifestyle and Zoroastrians traditionally sing, dance, play music and drink wine together during the celebrations in marked contrast to those around them.

In Zoroastrianism people are expected to act, for, ultimately, it is deeds which speak louder than thoughts and words. Connected with this, it is felt that to be able to make sound judgements, a healthy environment is needed. Therefore, purity or *asha* is to be observed with reference to the earth, the water and the air. Our concern not to pollute these elements also explains how our misunderstood funeral rite of exposure on mountain tops developed as a precursor to recycling through organ donation. It also explains why Zoroastrians chose not to wash in rivers or streams but to draw water off in vessels to be used elsewhere so that the flowing water which could be used downstream would not sullied by personal washing. Much importance is attached to the meritorious act of making infertile land abundant by bringing water to it, and making swampy waterlogged land fertile by draining it and planting crops. The environmental consciousness which pervades the religion accounts for the reputation Zoroastrians built up as excellent gardeners who knew how to irrigate in difficult conditions and how to produce abundance where others failed. Exhortations to a marrying couple include several about the desirability of cultivating land and at the birth of each child it is normal to plant a tree.

Within a healthy and well nurtured society, deeds above all else have to reflect the choice individuals make in following the path of purity or *asha*. Bodily cleanliness is one manifestation of this and the wearing of the white muslin undergarment, the *sedreh*, donned at the initiation ceremony of *sedreh pushi*, represents this, as it reflects purity and has to be worn spotless.

Hard Work and Charity

Zoroastrians are told in the *Gathas* that laziness and sloth are frowned on. It is our duty to toil, so that life may be enjoyed when relaxing after toil and when the bounty of our hard work produces fruit. Zoroastrians, furthermore, are exhorted to do good deeds and amongst these is the nurturing of a charitable disposition which inclines us to part with a little of what would otherwise be our own. In societies where agriculture is the principle source of income, memorial feasts, *gahambar*, in remembrance of the person who endowed the feast, are held annually and bread and dried fruits are distributed to the whole community, who are expected to participate, funded by the income from the sale of the land produce. In more industrial communities, and among more affluent families, it is more commonplace to find a person endowing a hospital, a home for the aged, or a school. Nowadays, endowments are also made for communities to meet at the local centre for a meal together after prayers of thanksgiving and remembrance.

In the rural communities that characterized Zoroastrian society, it was also a very frequent event to find charity stews being cooked on the street corner, or sweet, fried and spiced bread being handed out to passers by from groups of people cooking over fires outside their homes or at the cross roads. Candles would also sometimes appear in niches at street corners, all of these being acts of charity in differing measure according to the means of the person in question, offered as an act of thanksgiving for a piece of good fortune or an earlier imprecation being fulfilled. It should also be mentioned that it was often menfolk in the community who were the chief cooks, fire stokers and handlers of the vast cauldrons which had to be used to prepare community charity stews, while the women and children did the preparatory work.

Gender Equality

Equality of gender remains a feature which has singled out Zoroastrians from their Iranian compatriots throughout history. A woman's willingness to speak her views in the presence of her partner, and for those views to be accepted as valid, was characteristic and still is. In every sense the Zoroastrian woman has maintained her equality of position in society, and, where necessary, has been head of the household in the absence of her husband or, in the case of widowhood, has made decisions affecting land sales, inheritances, harvesting times, educational choices or marriage partners for offspring. Since the early twentieth century when girls' schools were opened for Zoroastrians, women have shown their competence in every sphere by achieving high qualifications and careers in all domains where men have succeeded.

There is, however, one issue which outsiders may raise in trying to make a case for the unequal treatment of women in Zoroastrianism and this concerns concepts of purity and pollution, which resulted from the entrenched dualism which had evolved by the last phase of Zoroastrianism under the Sassanians between the third and seventh centuries CE when the religion was already almost 2000 years old, the age of Christianity today. It was almost inevitable that by that time the original ideas should have undergone some permutations. In fact, some aspects of the original philosophy had been so elaborated that dualistic categories had been arranged for the classification of all material things. As a result of this, dirt, darkness, noxious creatures (e.g. scorpions, snakes etc.), death, blood, and so on were arranged in the negative or impure category and because women underwent monthly cycles, they were classified as impure during this time. This meant that members of the community were careful not to come into contact with them during this period and women withdrew on monthly 'sabbaticals' with their friends and family members to a special part of the household where they used special utensils and had no contact with those in the 'pure' category until they had finished their cycle and undergone ritual purification. It must be stressed that they were neither treated in an inferior way nor despised, but merely treated as different during this time of the month. This practice has all but died out although residual aspects may be detected in the unwillingness of some women to go to the temple at this time of the month out of respect for the sanctity and purity of the fire.

It may be of interest to note that Parsees, especially those raised in East Africa, tend to be more orthodox, inasmuch as they are more tenacious than their co-religionists from Bombay in maintaining traditions that they learnt in their family homes and in their religious centres. It was because of this same spirit of fidelity that Parsees who left Iran in the face of fierce persecution in the tenth century CE and were given permission to settle around Sanjan in Gujerat, India, decided to try and maintain what they remembered of their faith and practices. However, as they left Iran at a time of turmoil when much knowledge had been lost or distorted, just before the Arab conquest and certainly afterwards, what they preserved was not necessarily 'correct' or authentic. Meanwhile, the Iranians who did not convert to Islam, mainly humble people and priests, struggled in the face of intense persecution to maintain their traditions, and the spirit of their religious faith, which did not need texts but had permeated their lifestyles and outlook. Thus with Zoroastrians located in two centres from the tenth century, and with little contact between them until the last century, it is not surprising that certain beliefs and rituals evolved differently. Now, in diaspora, the Indian culture has re-met with its Iranian counterpart, and attempts are being made to bring the differing interpretations into line with each other. Iranian Zoroastrians cite numerous Zoroastrian texts written at differing times but above all the *Gathas* (attributed to the prophet) where several explicit lines indicate without a shadow of doubt, that the religion was open and given to those who embrace its ethics and values freely. The Orthodox Parsees are therefore having to re-think their rigid rejection of 'new' Zoroastrians as they cannot deny what is explicitly attributed to Zoroaster.

Naturally there is much more which could be said but I have brought forward the salient points. I hope that readers will now have a fuller understanding of the main principles and practices of the Zoroastrian faith.

For Further Information

1.   The Baha'is

a.   The Bahá'í Information Office
        27 Rutland Gate
        London SW7 1PD
        Tel: 020-7584 2566

b.   The Bahá'í Publishing Trust
        FREEPOST
        Oakham
        Rutland LE15 6BR
        Tel: 0800 0924149
        Tel: 01572 722780
        Fax: 01572 724280
        Email: bpt.sales@bahai.org.uk

2.   The Buddhists

a.   The Buddhist Society
        58 Eccleston Square
        London SW1V 1PH
        Tel: 020 7834 5858
        http:// www.buddsoc.org.uk

b.   The Network of Buddhist Organizations UK
        The Old Courthouse
        43 Renfrew Road
        Kennington
        London SE11 4NA
        Tel: 020 8682 3442

3.   The Hindus

a.   National Council of Hindu Temples
        c/o Shree Sanatan Mandir, Weymouth Street, off Catherine Street
        Leicester
        Leicestershire
        LE4 6FP

b.   ISKON Educational Services
        Bhaktivedanta Manor
        Hilfield Lane
        Aldenham
        Watford
        Hertfordshire WD2 8EZ

c.   Vishwa Hindu Parishad
        48 Wharfedale Gardens
        Thornton Heath
        Croydon CR7 6LB

4.   The Jains

        The Jain Centre
        32 Oxford Street
        Leicester LE1 5XU
        tel. 0116 2543091

5.   The Jews

a.   Board of Deputies of British Jews
        5th floor, Commonwealth House, 1-19 New Oxford St.
        London WC1A 1NF
        tel. 020-7543-5400
        E-mail: info@bod.org.uk

b.   For more detailed documents and reports on British & World Jewry:
        The Institute for Jewish Policy Research
        79 Wimpole St.
        London W1G 9RY
        tel. 020-7935-8266
        fax. 020-7935-3252
        E-mail: jpr@jpr.org.uk

c.   The Council of Christians and Jews
        5th Floor, Camelford House
        89 Albert Embankment
        London SE1 7TP
        tel. 020-7820-0090
        fax 020-7820-0504
        E-mail: ccjuk@aol.com

d.   For opportunities to engage in further study:

        Centre for Jewish-Christian Relations
        Wesley House, Jesus Lane
        Cambridge CB5 8BJ
        tel. 01223-741048/9
        E-mail: enquiries@cjcr.cam.ac.uk

        Open Learning Centre
        Cliff College, Calver, Hope Valley, nr Sheffield S32 3XG
        tel. 01246-582321
        fax. 01246-583739

6.   The Muslims

a.   The Islamic Foundation
Ratby Lane
Markfield
Leicester
LE67 9RN
tel. 01530 244946
(publishes *Encounters: Journal of Inter-Cultural Perspectives* and has an active interest in inter-faith work)

b.   Muslim College
20-22 Creffield Road
London W5 3RP
tel. 020 8992 6636
(offers some courses for those who are not Muslims)

c.   The London Central Mosque and Islamic Cultural Centre
146 Park Road
London NW8 7RG
tel. 020 7724 3363

7.   New Agers

1.   INFORM (Information Network Focus on New Religious Movements)
Houghton Street
London WC2A 2AE
tel. 020 7955 7654
E-mail: inform@lse.ac.uk

8.   The Sikhs

a.   The Sikh Missionary Society
10 Featherstone Road
Southall
Middlesex UB2 5AA

b.   The Sikh Education Council
14 Brightside Road
Leicester
LE5 5LD

9.   The Zoroastrians

a.   World Zoroastrian Organization
135 Tennison Road
South Norwood
London SE25 5NF

Further Reading

General Introductions and Resource Books on World Religions

Ed. John Bowker, *The Oxford Dictionary of World Religions,* Oxford University Press, 1997
Ed. John R. Hinnells, *Handbook of Living Religions*, Penguin, Second Edition, 1995
Ninian Smart, *The World's Religions,* Cambridge University Press, 1989
Huston Smith, *The World's Religions,* Harper Collins, 1991
Ed. R.C. Zaehner, *The Concise Encyclopedia of Living Faiths,* Hutchinson, 1971

Inter-Faith Relations

Wesley Ariarajah, *The Bible and People of Other Faiths,* Geneva, World Council of Churches, 1985
Wesley Ariarajah, *Not Without My Neighbour: Issues in Inter-Faith Relations,* Geneva, World Council of Churches, 1999
Peter Bishop, *The Christian and People of Other Faiths,* Peterborough, Epworth, 1997
Peter Bishop, *Written on the Flyleaf: A Christian Faith in the Light of Other Faiths*, Peterborough, Epworth, 1998
Kenneth Cracknell, *Justice, Courtesy and Love: Theologians and Missionaries Encountering World Religions 1846-1914,* Peterborough, Epworth, 1995
Maureen Henderson, *Friends Along the Way*, Peterborough, Epworth, 1999
Michael Nazir Alli, *Citizens and Exiles*, London, SPCK, 1998
John Sanders, *No Other Name, London*, SPCK, 1994

Baha'is

Writings of Bahá'u'lláh

There are several editions of each of Bahá'u'lláh's major works as well as a large number of thematic compilations, so it is worth checking with the Bahá'í Publishing Trust what they have available. These may include the following:

* *The Hidden Words* – a collection of poetic epigrams which convey the heart of Bahá'u'lláh's spiritual and ethical teachings.
* *Gleanings from the Writings of Bahá'u'lláh* – a compilation of essential passages from Bahá'u'lláh's major works; all the important themes in his writings are to be found here.
* *Remembrance of God: A Selection of Bahá'í Prayers and Holy Writings*, Bahá'í Publishing Trust, India
* *The Bahá'ís,* Bahá'í International Community. (This profile of the Bahá'í community world-wide, its beliefs, practices and geographical spread comes in the form of a large-format, glossy colour magazine.)

Moojan Momen, *The Bahá'í Faith: A Short Introduction,* Oxford, Oneworld
Mary Perkins, *Day of Glory: The Life of Bahá'u'lláh,* published by George Ronald
Joseph Shepherd, *The Elements of the Bahá'í Faith,* Element Books
Michael Sours, *The Station and Claims of Bahá'u'lláh*, US Bahá'í Publishing Trust

Buddhists

Eds. Heinz Bechert & Richard Gombrich, *The World of Buddhism,* Thames & Hudson, 1984 (1993)

M. Carrithers, *The Buddha*, Oxford University Press, 1983

Rupert Gethin, *The Foundations of Buddhism*, Oxford University Press, 1998

Elizabeth J Harris, *What Buddhists Believe,* Oxford, Oneworld, 1998 (reissued 2000)

Peter Harvey, *An Introduction to Buddhism,* Cambridge University Press, 1990

Aloysius Pieris, S.J. *Love Meets Wisdom: A Christian Experience of Buddhism,* Maryknoll, Orbis, 1988

Walpola Rahula, *What the Buddha Taught,* Oneworld, Oxford, 1997 (reprint)

Hindus

Ed. R. Ballard, *Desh pardesh: the South Asian Experience in Britain*, London, Hurst, 1994

Swami A.C. Bhaktivedanta, *Bhagavad-Gita as it is*, Letchmore Heath, Bhaktivedanta Book Trust, 1975

J.L. Brockington, *Hinduism and Christianity,* London, Macmillan, 1992

C.J. Fuller, *The Camphor Flame:Popular Hinduism & Society in India,* New Jersey, Princeton University Press, 1992

Gavin Flood, *An Introduction to Hinduism,* Cambridge University Press, 1996

E. Jackson. & D. Killingley, *Approaches to Hinduism*, World Religions in Education, with lists of resources for Teachers, London, J.Murray, 1992

K.K. Klostermaier, *A Survey of Hinduism*, State of New York University Press ,1994, 2nd edition

Kim Knott, *Hinduism: A Short Introduction*, Oxford University Press, 1998

Julius Lipner, *Hindus: their religious beliefs and practices*, London, Routledge, 1995

Ed. Gwyneth Little, *Meeting Hindus*, Leicester, Christians Aware, 2001

R. Panikkar, *The Vedic Experience: An Anthology of the Vedas for Modern Man & Contemporary Celebration,* London, Darton, Longman & Todd, 1977

Eric Lott, *Vedantic Approaches to God,* London, Macmillan, 1986

Vishwa Hindu Parishad (U.K.), *Explaining Hindu Dharma: A Guide to Teachers* London, Vishwa Hindu Parishad

Muslims

A Ahmed, *Discovering Islam,* London, Routledge, 1988

A.J. Arberry, *The Qur'an Interpreted,* OUP World Classics

John Bowker J, *What Muslims Believe*, Oxford, Oneworld, Reissued 2000

Martin Forward M, *Muhammad: A Short Biography,* Oxford, Oneworld, 1997

Geoffrey Parrinder, *Jesus in the Qur'an,* Oxford, Oneworld, 1995

W. M. Watt, *A Short History of Islam*, Oxford, Oneworld, 1995

W.M. Watt, *Muhammad, Prophet and Statesman,* Oxford University Press

Recommended by the London Central Mosque and Islamic Cultural Centre which also gave permission for its photographs to be used to illustrate the original article in the Methodist Recorder:

Hammudah Abdalati, *Islam in Focus*, the Islamic Cultural Centre: 146 Park Road, London NW8 7RG

Martin Lings, *Mohammad: His Life Based on the Earliest Sources,* The Islamic Texts Society: Cambridge 1983 (1997)

The Jains

Marcus Banks, *Organising Jainism in India and England*, Clarendon Press.
Michael Carrithers and Caroline Humphrey, *The Assembly of Listeners – Jains in Society*, Cambridge University Press.
Paul Dundas, *The Jains*, London, Routledge, 1992.
Padmanabh S Jaini, *The Jaina Path of Purification*, University of California Press.
James Laidlow, *Riches and Renunciation – Religion, Economy and Society among the Jains*, Oxford University Press.
Paul Marett, *Jainism Explained*, Jain Samaj Europe, Leicester.
Pratapaditya Pal, *The Peaceful Liberators – Jain Art from India*, Thames and Hudson, 1994.

The Jews

Judaism in Britain

Order the weekly *Jewish Chronicle* at your local newsagents.
Books by Jonathan Sacks e.g. *Faith in the Future*, Dartman, Longman and Todd, 1995.
Statistics cited in the article come from the current *Jewish Year Book* published annually by Valentine Mitchell in association with the *Jewish Chronicle* at Newbury House, 900 Eastern Ave. London IG2 7HH

What Jews believe

D. Cohn-Sherbok, *The Jewish Faith*, SPCK, 1993
Nicholas de Lange, *Judaism,* Oxford University Press
C. M. Pilkington, *Teach Yourself Judaism,* Hodder & Stoughton

Israel / Palestine

Colin Chapman, *Whose Promised Land?* Lion, 1992
D. Cohn-Sherbok, *Israel - the history of an idea*, SPCK, 1992
Kenneth Cragg, *Palestine - the prize and price of Zion*, Cassell, 1997

Christian-Jewish issues

Marcus Braybrooke, *Time to meet,*SCM, 1990
Helen P. Fry, *Christian-Jewish Dialogue: A reader,* University of Exeter Press, 1996
Hans Ucko, *Common roots - new horizons*, Geneva, World Council of Churches, 1994

The New Age

Eileen Barker, *New Religious Movements,* HMSO, 1995
Ed. W Bloom and Button, *The Seeker's Guide: a New Age Resource Book*, London, Aquarian Press/Thorsons
Paul Heelas, *The New Age Movement*, Oxford, Blackwell, 1996
Rachel Storm, *In Search of Heaven on Earth*, London, Aquarian Press, 1992

The Sikhs

Ed. Joy Barrow, *Meeting Sikhs,* Leicester, Christians Aware, 1999
Ed. Kerry Brown, *Sikh Art and Literature*, London, Routledge, 1999
W. Owen Cole, *Teach Yourself Sikhism*, Hodder and Stoughton, 1994
W. Owen Cole and Piara Singh Sambhi, *Sikhism and Christianity: A Comparative Study*, Macmillan, 1993
Ed. and Trans.W H. McLeod, *Textual Sources for the Study of Sikhism,* Chicago, University of Chicago Press, 1990
W.H. McLeod, *Sikhism*, Penguin Books, 1997

Zoroastrians

Mary Boyce, *Zoroastrians*, London, Routledge Kegan & Paul, 1978
Farhang Mehr, *The Zoroastrian Tradition*, Element, 1991

The Contributors

JOY BARROW is Head of Religious Education at a high school in west London and has a doctorate in Sikhism through the University of Leeds. She is also a visiting lecturer at Roehampton Institute of Higher Education, editor of *Meeting Sikhs*, published by Christians Aware and Consultant on Sikhism and Education for the Methodist Church.

SHAHIN BEKHRADNIA, a Zoroastrian of the Iranian tradition, is a teacher of ancient history and classical civilisation, a Justice of the Peace and a legal consultant. She has written and published on Zoroastrianism, including a post-graduate thesis in anthropology on issues of Zoroastrian identity in the twentieth century, and is active in inter-faith movements and organisations.

DAVID CRAIG was for many years head of religious programmes within the BBC World Service. He is an adviser to the Centre for Jewish-Christian Relations in Cambridge and also to Multi-Faith Net, an initiative of the University of Derby. He is now Secretary for Communications at the United Society for the Propagation of the Gospel.

MARTIN EGGLETON, Methodist minister, is chaplain of a Methodist School. Previous to this, he was a chaplain at the University of Middlesex, where he also taught New Age Religion. He is a Governor of INFORM (Information Network Focus On Religious Movements) and consultant on New Age and New Religious Movements for the Methodist Church.

ELIZABETH HARRIS is Secretary for Inter-Faith Relations within the Methodist Church in Britain. She has a doctorate in Buddhist studies and has taught Buddhism at Westminster College, Oxford. She is author of *What Buddhists Believe* (Oneworld, 1998) and co-editor of *Meeting Buddhists*, published by Christians Aware.

MICHAEL IPGRAVE is Secretary of the Churches' Commission on Inter Faith Relations within Churches Together in Britain and Ireland and Inter Faith Adviser to the General Synod of the Church of England. He has specialised in the study of Jainism and maintains close links with the Jain community in the UK.

BARNABAS LEITH is Secretary General of the Bahá'í Community of the United Kingdom. He is a former Chair of the United Kingdom and Ireland Chapter of the World Conference on Religion and Peace.

ERIC LOTT was a missionary in India for thirty years, including many years as Professor of Indian Studies at the United Theological College, Bangalore. He has written and published on Hinduism and returns to India annually to lecture on the subject. He has been a Consultant on Hinduism for the Methodist Church.

NICK SISSONS is a Methodist minister in Llandudno. For many years, he has been involved in Jewish-Christian dialogue. He is author of the course on Judaism offered by the Open Learning Centre of the Methodist Church, a member of the Council of Christians and Jews and Consultant on Judaism for the Methodist Church.